Anthony Giddens

This book provides an introduction to the work of Anthony
Giddens, and a critical discussion of his ideas. It sets out the
background to and sources for Giddens's development of structuration theory and describes the main features of this theory. The
author also discusses the substantive contributions that Giddens
has made to the theory of social class and his historical sociology,
including his conception of modernity.

The book is intended to provide an accessible introduction to
Giddens's work and also to situate structuration theory in the
context of other approaches. It is argued that while Giddens has
made some important contributions to social theory, structuration theory is not the transcendent grand theory that it is
sometimes claimed to be. It does not replace other approaches
nor does it incorporate some of the more important insights of
modern philosophy and psychotherapy.

It is the only book (so far) to deal with Giddens's work as a
whole which avoids the vexing extremes of hagiography and
facile criticism. Judicious, crisply argued and highly readable,
the book will be of interest to students of Sociology and those
working in the other Social Sciences.

Ian Craib lectures in Sociology at the University of Essex and
works as a group psychotherapist.

Anthony Giddens

Ian Craib

London and New York

First published in 1992
by Routledge
11 New Fetter Lane, London EC4P 4EE

Simultaneously published in the USA and Canada
by Routledge
a division of Routledge, Chapman and Hall Inc.
29 West 35th Street, New York, NY 10001

© 1992 Ian Craib

Typeset in Baskerville by Witwell Ltd, Southport
Printed and bound in Great Britain by
Mackays of Chatham PLC, Chatham, Kent

British Library Cataloguing in Publication Data
Craib, Ian *1945–*
   Anthony Giddens.
   1. Sociology
   I. Title
   301.092

Library of Congress Cataloging in Publication Data
Craib, Ian 1945–
   Anthony Giddens/Ian Craib.
   p.   cm.
   Includes bibliographical references and index.
   1. Giddens, Anthony.   2. Sociology-Methodology.   3. Social
structure.   4. Sociology-Great Britain.   I. Title
   HM22.G8G5434   1991
   301'.01–dc20   91-12147
                                                              CIP

ISBN 0-415-07072-4 (hbk)
ISBN 0-415-02814-0 (pbk)

For Fiona, Ben, Chris, Penelope and Theo: without whom this book would have been finished six months earlier, and the author's life impoverished beyond imagination.

Contents

Preface

I have found this a very difficult book to write. I do not think in the same way as Anthony Giddens, and have had to spend much time thinking against myself. I hope the result is at least fair to its subject.

I suspect that more people than I would like to acknowledge have had to tolerate me whilst I have been writing; those I would like to acknowledge include David Lee, of the Sociology Department at Essex, who read and discussed a long and remarkably tedious first draft; Professor Christopher Bryant, of Salford, for some generous comments on the same draft, and Rob Stones, also of the Sociology Department at Essex, for reading a later draft, arguing with me, and making me think.

Chapter 1

Out of chaos?

THE GIDDENS PROJECT

Anthony Giddens is certainly a phenomenon amongst British sociologists : a major 'grand theorist'. Increasingly, he has come to see himself as a social, rather than just a sociological theorist, concerned with ideas relevant across the range of social sciences and breaking down the barriers amongst the disciplines. The volume of secondary literature now appearing – four substantial books alone in the year around my writing these words[1] – is a tribute to his importance in modern sociology. He is *the* main interpreter of modern social theory, and not only in the English-speaking world. This demands both an accessible account of his work and a critical discussion, and this book attempts both. This chapter will be concerned with an initial characterisation of his enterprise and an outline of the central threads of my critical discussion.

His project has unfolded in a consistent way since *Capitalism and Modern Social Theory* was published in 1971. What strikes me about this book now, looking at it from nearly twenty years on, is that it is possible to pick out two strands of Giddens's thought which interweave throughout his work: the nature of a general social theory on the one hand, and understanding the development of modern industrial society on the other. Marx, Weber and Durkheim were, he argues, primarily concerned with what distinguishes capitalism from other preceding forms of social organisation, and his comparison of the three emphasises the centrality to each of changing social relationships. It is misleading to treat them as if they were producing general, universally applicable theories of society: doing so has left sociology in a strait-jacket.

The central object of sociology should be modern society and the changes it is undergoing. Instead of taking each theorist as providing a theoretical paradigm, we need to subject them to criticism, keeping what is useful to this task and abandoning the rest. In particular, we should sort out what it was in their work which was a result of and a response to conditions that no longer exist. Social theory has to be radically restructured if we are to understand the modern world. Giddens's next important book, *The Class Structure of the Advanced Societies* in 1973, was concerned with modern social change, but from then through to the first volume of *A Contemporary Critique of Historical Materialism* in 1981, his work was almost entirely of a theoretical nature, and while much of his output remains theoretical, there has now been a return to understanding the nature of modern society and social change.

It is difficult to characterise his enterprise in any easy way. It is a radical revision of social theory and of sociology itself, which increasingly extends to the other social sciences, as he writes about history, geography and economics. It is a work of synthesis, bringing together insights from many different disciplines and thinkers; it is, I think, symptomatic that one of his most recent publications has been a text book, which carries implications of an established body of knowledge and research, a solid discipline, which up to now very few people have thought sociology to be. For the time being, however, I will concentrate on the radical reconstruction of social theory: that is the centre of his work.

Giddens has often catalogued the situation from which this project appeared. There was after the Second World War a period of twenty years or more when sociology was dominated by what he calls an 'orthodox consensus', when the dominant theoretical framework was Parsons' structural-functionalism. During the late 1960s, this began to break down under the impact of external political events and there was a period, the effects of which are still very clearly with us, when sociology fragmented, searching through politics and philosophy in particular for the means to grasp what seemed a rapidly changing world. Giddens, whose main work began to appear well into this period, offers a way out of the chaos. In addition to the revision of the classic sociological thinkers, he offers a rewriting of the history of sociology, criticising what he often calls the 'myths' of sociology: that social science can model itself on the natural sciences; that it has its origins in conservative thought; that sociology can be seen as a debate between 'consensus' and 'conflict' approaches and others.

The last of these is particularly important. On a much deeper level Giddens is offering a solution to divisions which have plagued sociological thought, especially that between 'structure' and 'action'. It has always been common, with justification, to distinguish between those approaches to sociology which concentrate on identifying and understanding enduring patterns of human relationships – often seen as independent of our perceptions and as determinants of our actions – and those which look at individual and collective human actions and concern themselves only with the way people think about, see and act in the world. In place of this he offers *structuration theory*, which tries to approach both structure and action within one coherent theoretical framework.

This theory has been formulated in different ways, but increasingly by Giddens himself and by those who find his work most useful, as involving a change in our conception of what sociology is and what it studies. In *The Constitution of Society* (1984), his most systematic statement of structuration theory, he identifies his concern with a shift from epistemology to ontology. The former is concerned with the grounds of our knowledge, and Giddens is implying that sociology has concerned itself too much with the issue of producing adequate knowledge, at the expense of looking at the real nature of the social world and what it is studying, i.e. ontology. Placing his theory in the context, not of action and structure, but the individual and society, he argues that these are in fact secondary concerns:

> The basic domain of study of the social sciences, according to the theory of structuration, is neither the experience of the individual actor, nor the existence of any form of societal totality, but social practices ordered across space and time.
>
> (Giddens 1984: 2)

The old dualisms – action/structure, individual/society, determinism/voluntarism – should be reconceived as *dualities*; in other words, instead of separate and opposing things in the world or as mutually exclusive ways of thinking about the world, they are simply two sides of the same coin. If we look at social practices in one way, we can see actors and actions; if look at them another way we can see structures.

This theory of structuration is built up through a long process of critique and synthesis. Several targets stand out: positivism, functionalism and evolutionary theory are unreservedly attacked, but often criticisms take a positive form. Modern linguistic philosophy, structuralism and post-structuralism, critical theory, Marxism, modern human geography and many other approaches are criticised, but in each case ideas and concepts are taken from them to contribute to structuration theory. Giddens recognises that often he employs concepts in a very different way to their original use, but seems to think that the advantages of doing this outweigh the disadvantages. One of the beneficial effects of this is that he has introduced and given respectability to many import-ant theorists and ideas that were, twenty years ago, only on the fringes of sociology. A sense of how radical his introduction of these ideas seems can be gleaned from the less than enthusiastic comments of sociologists from the 'old' mainstream of British sociology: John Rex (1983), Peter Worsley and Mick Mann (see Mullan 1987).

THE DIFFICULTY OF READING GIDDENS

This has not been an easy book to write. At times, it has left me irritable, frustrated and disoriented. Having long been accus-tomed to the chaos of sociology, I have found the same chaos intensified to an exquisite and almost unbearable degree in Giddens's attempts to organise it. At other times, it has been exciting, thought provoking, and immensely stimulating. I have come out of it knowing much more than when I started.

Similar reactions are reflected in other commentaries on his work: he is described as 'foxlike', a 'honey-bee' flitting from theory to theory, and 'quintessentially post-modernist'; reading his work is like 'trying to catch quicksilver'. There are debates about whether his work is systematic, eclectic or simply syncretic (a nasty word, meaning accepting incompatible positions). Some years ago, I published a paper (Craib 1986) criticising Giddens as if he were a systematic theorist. It is only recently that I have realised that he is not, or rather, not quite. There are certainly systematising aspects of his work, not least in the constant series of classifications and diagrams that fill his books. Yet his synthesis of approaches is not bound together through a logical or rational system, as we have come to expect from theorists such as Parsons and many modern Marxists. Concepts are added and developed because they fill gaps in the description of the world, not because they derive from each other and identify causal mechanisms. I think it is the peculiar way he builds up his synthesis, through a range of borrowings and changes of meaning, that makes him difficult to read and gives rise to the debate. Zygmunt Bauman describes him correctly, and pointedly, as being 'non-partisan in his partisanship': he sees himself most often as not arguing for a particular position but drawing all positions together. I often find myself lost in the ingredients, reacting as I would perhaps if I found custard on my lamb chops.

The result is that when reading his work, I am constantly impressed. His summaries and discussions of other thinkers are clear, precise and acute and I often find myself referring students to them as one of the best possible secondary sources. As he builds up his own position, he makes many stimulating and intelligent points. Yet at the end, I do not quite know where I am, or what I am left with. The answer is a range of concepts that can be applied in a variety of situations, but it is always difficult to identify when and where application is appropriate or what can be learnt from it. Richard Bernstein has pointed out that in this respect he is not unique amongst sociologists:

> Giddens is guilty of a 'sin' common among other sociologists who think in a grand manner. For whenever he confronts a difficult problem, he is tempted to introduce a plethora of distinctions and schemas. Many . . . are illuminating, but one frequently has the uneasy feeling that much more needs to be said about the *criteria* of their applicability.
>
> (Held and Thompson 1989: 27)

Nor, of course, are his concerns as original as he sometimes seems to think. Parsons, a central target, aimed also at overcoming the dualism of action and structure and as Giddens himself points out, the fact that such a dualism has been central to sociology's understanding of itself means that he is concerned with problems as old as sociology.

Understanding this has helped me to understand his writings, as has my realisation that he is offering a theory which describes the world rather than explains it. His own description of his theory as 'sensitising' is also helpful. This is the way that Herbert Blumer (1969) describes symbolic interactionism: it is not a theory aimed at telling us what happens in the world, or explaining what happens, but it gives us a broad idea of what we might be looking for and some ways of thinking about it. Ira Cohen (1989), one of Giddens's most enthusiastic commentators, elaborates on this: Giddens is concerned with the openness of history and of human action, its non-determined nature, and a closed, deductive theory can blind us to that.

THE GIDDENS PHENOMENON

Until Giddens, there had been no major social theorist with an international reputation produced from the ranks of British sociology; it had remained firmly rooted in a strong empirical tradition, with occasional snipes at 'grand theory' – as witnessed by the reactions I mentioned earlier. Perry Anderson (1968) argues that the origins of this lie in the peculiar nature of the British class structure, that there had been no social or political dynamic pushing a social class into the development of a totalising social theory. It is certainly the case that class relations have become more polarised in Britain over the twenty-five years that Giddens has been writing, and that in particular this period has seen Marxism taken seriously by British academics, if not for the first time, then on a scale not equalled before. The develop-ment of Giddens's work has to be set in this context, but other contexts are important as well: the development of British sociology as an institution, and the rapidly changing nature of the modern world.

My comments about sociology are impressionistic. The 1960s and early '70s were a period of often rapid expansion. When I took my first degree (1967–70) few of my teachers had taken sociology degrees; even now, looking at my colleagues, I can see a social psychologist, a psychologist, a philosopher, an economist and a social historian, all of whom came through to sociology during that period. Because it was an expanding discipline, promotion could be easy and fast, and it was possible to make a name for oneself fairly rapidly. The best way to make a name for oneself is to attack the previous generation and offer something new and radical which appears to sweep aside old problems. There is something about the growth of sociology over that period, in the enthusiasm it sparked in students, in the way in which it saw the world, which was imperialist. We did not see ourselves as working within a limited scientific endeavour, seeking to understand some limited part of the social world; rather we saw ourselves as trying to understand the whole world, covering everything from the theory of knowledge to the understanding of the minor details of everyday life and conversation.

My view of all this is that sociology developed pretensions beyond its age, in fact pretensions beyond what is possible for it as a discipline. I do not think it is possible to develop one all-embracing theory of the social world: that world is made up of many different phenomena which do not fit together even into a 'contradictory whole', and there is no one totalising theory to embrace them. Nevertheless sociology did, and to some extent still does, tend to behave as though this were possible.

Giddens's work belongs in this context. I should make it clear that I am not being critical of Giddens or sociology in moral terms. The expansion of higher education in general and sociology in particular enabled the exercise of normal human ambition, and those who grasped the opportunity were without doubt worthy of the success they achieved. I am critical in intellectual terms, however, in that it seems to me that sociology does generate over-ambitious attempts at intellectual understanding and explanation. Sociologists can believe that we can or have solved philosophical and intellectual problems that have always plagued human knowledge.

This leads me to the wider society. A constant theme throughout my critical discussions in this book will be the experience we have of living in modern societies, and it is in fact the specific and unique nature of modern society that Giddens is concerned with. That experience, I will argue, is one of increasing fragmentation, threat, instability and confusion. It is to Giddens's credit that he so often speaks to these issues directly. In our everyday world, this experience demands an answer, some sort of solution which can ease the tension, and I think perhaps that the totalising attempts of sociology can be seen as one way in which our culture responds. I shall argue that, like many of our individual attempts, it is a defensive strategy which denies and glosses over the reality with which we are faced.

LINES OF CRITICISM

My critical discussion of Giddens's work will be around the
theme of the complexity of the social world and the impossibility
of building any one theory to encompass it, even within the
limits of sociology, let alone the social sciences in general.
Acknowledging this is, I think, for sociologists in particular, a
painful task. It is not dissimilar to the task I witness in my other
role, as a psychotherapist, when individuals have to come to
terms with aspects of their selves and situations that they find
difficult to accept. What I find intriguing is that the same tactics
often used in theory are used by individuals in practice to deny
these realities.

When reading Giddens, I often find myself falling back on my
own pre-established ideas and simply asserting my position
against his. Several of the critical commentaries do this, and I
think it is a particularly sterile form of criticism: 'I don't like
your toys, mine are better.' I can't find a way to avoid this; clearly
I do think my toys are better, otherwise I would get rid of them.
However, the grounds on which I wish to keep them is that they
open up the possibilities for playing; we can get more fun out of
them. It is as if Giddens is saying that all the modern child needs
is Lego; a dextrous use of Lego will satisfy our creative, learning
and recreational requirements. My position is that I am happy to
play with Lego, but I want to hold on to my meccano, wooden
blocks, ghostbuster figures and the bits and pieces I've picked up
from local junk heaps. And, what's more, I don't want them
sorted into neat little piles according to colour, size and shape; I
want to keep them jumbled up in my one big box. However
chaotic sociology may at times appear, the pain of the chaos is
worthwhile for what we can produce from it.

My critical discussion of Giddens will take place along a
number of interrelated lines.

Ontological depth

It seems to me insufficient to see sociology, and the social
sciences in general, as dealing with only one type of phenomenon: social practices. The social world is, on the face of it, littered
with different types of things: people, institutions, the solid
inanimate matter we make buildings out of, and so on. More

particularly I remain convinced by the notion that there are such things as underlying social structures, which are not easily visible, except in their effects, but have a different type of existence to the individuals who inhabit them and to the practices of those individuals. In other words, I think that the structure/action divide in sociology is there for a very good reason: the social world is made up of, amongst other things, structure and action, and these two are not the same.

I also think that the notion of 'ontological depth', real underlying social structures, different to Giddens's conception, enables some basis for understanding the apparent fragmentation of modern life that, I will argue, Giddens cannot grasp but reproduces in his theory. As I write this, I am increasingly aware that it is a matter of assertion. The state of the advanced societies is such that it is often no longer possible to believe that there is some coherent order to society and history, without looking, certainly without feeling, foolish. My argument is that we cannot assert any knowledge of that order, but to engage in social analysis at all, we have to assume that perhaps such an order is there to be discovered. The possibility of there being some underlying social structure and historical process seems to share the status of Pascal's hidden god, and if sometimes I tend to favour a Marxist framework, it is less because I believe it is right than because I believe it is the best we have, and that it fails in more interesting ways than the other alternatives. Much modern theory, including some varieties of Marxism and everything that falls under the heading of post-structuralism, has become bound up with the process of fragmentation in surrendering ideas of an underlying order or structure. The possibility of finding meaning in life recedes. It seems to me that it is a qualitatively different matter to give up the idea of meaning, as opposed to accepting that its discovery is becoming increasingly complex and difficult and acknowledging that any meaning will be a process and subject to disintegration and change. I will argue that in important ways, Giddens glosses over or cannot grasp these issues.

Theoretical pluralism

It should be apparent from this that I am opposed to synthetic exercises in social theory; or at least to synthetic attempts that claim to be more than another approach. There are two sets of arguments here. The first has to with the messiness of the real world and the unproductive nature of attempts to deal with this by curing it. The second is more directly concerned with epistemology, and with Paul Feyerabend's argument in *Against Method* (1975), in which he proposes an 'anarchist theory of knowledge' with the one rule 'anything goes'.

It often seems to me that Giddens produces a theoretical meld in which all differences disappear, and this is in part his intention. He often speaks of problems as if they are there to be solved rather than worked with. My fundamental objection to this is that I do not think it is the way that social theory should be carried out, that it is not theoretical work to solve problems or to bring things together; or at least some part of theoretical work might be concerned with doing these things but it is also theoretical work to create problems and take things apart – this is the aspect that is missing in Giddens. New knowledge emerges from a range of activities; general synthetic theories close down the possibilities of investigation and explanation that are open to us. Theoretical work comes to be like putting together a jigsaw puzzle: before we start, we already know what the final picture will be like.

In *Social Theory and Modern Sociology* (1987a), where Giddens predicts a growing theoretical synthesis in sociology (along the general lines, of course, of his own position), he mentions Feyerabend and concedes that sociology will always be variegated because of its intimate connection with social processes and conflicts; but this is not Feyerabend's point. The point is about discovery and creativity and the way they employ apparently strange or perhaps even wrong ideas. It is about the need for bits and pieces from the local junk heaps.

Modernity and fragmentation

I have mentioned this theme several times. I have indicated my general approval of chaos on a theoretical level, but it seems to me that the fragmentation of our experience in modern life is much more destructive. I shall develop a number of critical arguments around this. On one level, Giddens's work is about this fragmentation, an attempt to make sense of it, but an attempt that fails. At the same time, it is a denial of important elements of that experience: the theory simply cannot see them or rules them out of court. I shall argue that structuration theory is also a product and a refraction of social fragmentation.

Critical theory

Giddens often talks about social theory as critical theory, and he offers a number of analyses of the ways in which it is critical. I shall argue that there is no real basis for the development of a critical theory in his work. For me, one of the things that makes sociology and social theory worthwhile is that it can address the problems of human suffering in such a way as to make more sense of suffering than there was before, and to give meaning to that suffering, at least to the extent of seeing it in the context of a world that could be different. Without this, sociology does become sterile - both in terms of its ability to produce knowledge and the contribution it might make towards social change. My fear is that Giddens's work moves towards this ineffectiveness.

THE STRUCTURE OF THE BOOK

I have spent some time talking about my criticisms of Giddens, and I will extend them to inordinate length later. In general the structure of this book will be the structure of the standard student essay: an exposition and a criticism and a conclusion. I do not want to imply that the exposition is unimportant. Certainly for me it has been a considerable task to make sense of, be fair to and organise Giddens's thought in a way that might be helpful to others. I am by no means sure that I have succeeded; Giddens covers himself well, and I find it difficult to keep his theory in my head, or even in notes - it *is* rather like trying to grasp quicksilver.

I will start by looking at the ingredients of his synthesis, those he rejects and those he modifies and incorporates, giving greater attention than I have done so far to the context in which he was writing. There are then two long chapters of exposition. The first builds up an outline of structuration theory, beginning with Giddens's conception of agency, and practices, moving on to his notion of structure and the duality of structures; and then to a series of concepts he develops to look at different aspects of social processes, amongst which his notions of systems and institutions and of the importance of time and space are particularly significant. The second will present an account of his analysis of the development and nature of modern society, beginning with the early *The Class Structure of the Advanced Societies* (1973) and moving on through the two volumes of *A Contemporary Critique of Historical Materialism* (1981a and 1985a) to *The Consequences of Modernity* (1990). A shorter chapter will look at the relationship between structuration theory, empirical research and critical theory.

Finally, there will be a series of critical chapters dealing primarily with Giddens's theory rather than his historical sociology and following the lines I have already discussed. Much of these chapters pull together and organise criticisms that are scattered throughout the literature; my own contribution is the critique of Giddens's conception of the social actor and the personality. The tone of these chapters is, in fact, highly critical, and I have become reluctant to leave the issue there. Bryant and Jary (1991) comment on the reluctance of many British sociologists to recognise that British sociology has produced a 'star'; I wonder if part of that reluctance comes from envy – Giddens has perhaps realised the fantasies of many of us who committed ourselves to sociology during the period of intense and exciting debate out of which structuration theory developed. When I read my own criticisms of him, I can hear, in the background, my disillusion with my own earlier ideals for sociology. Whilst maintaining my criticisms, I would not want my disillusion to convey the impression that Giddens's attempt is not worthwhile, immensely stimulating and very important. The final chapter will tackle these aspects directly. A paradox of anything goes is that anything goes.

NOTE

1 See I. Cohen (1989), Held and Thompson (1989), Clarke *et al.* (1990), Bryant and Jary (1991).

Chapter 2

The theoretical omelette

This chapter is intended to provide a background to Giddens's development of structuration theory, looking in rather more detail at his views of what sociology is about and the way it has developed, his criticisms of the 'orthodox consensus' which began to break down in the mid-1960s, and the sources from which he develops his own ideas.

The omelette analogy seems to me appropriate. We cook an omelette when we are hungry, and given that we've got some eggs, we can add all sorts of usual, conventional and unusual ingredients, and we can prepare the ingredients in various ways, use different parts, peel or not peel the mushrooms. We don't have to worry too much about whether the finished product looks good and attractive, as long as it doesn't revolt the person who makes it, and we don't worry too much about hygiene when we cook it.

What makes Giddens hungry is the understanding of social change in the modern world. The eggs are the achievements of sociology, some of which he thinks have gone bad over the last century. These he wishes to reject, whilst he also wants to add a range of unexpected, novel ingredients and prepare some old ingredients in a new way. If we read the classical theorists as providing general theories of society – as arguing, for example, about economic determinism – we will not get very far. The most interesting features of the work of Marx, Weber and Durkheim are their attempts to identify what distinguished capitalism from previous forms of society.

If we focus on this common concern, we can see the inadequacies of the conventional ways of characterising the history of sociology. There is no great divide occurring around the end of the nineteenth century between a scientific sociology (Weber and Durkheim) and a pre-scientific social philosophy (Marx); nor is it the case that this period saw the development of a bourgeois sociology in opposition to Marxism. Further, it is not the case that sociology had its origins in conservative thought: in *Studies in Social and Political Theory* (1977), Giddens shows the radical aspects of Durkheim, the thinker most often marked off as an arch-conservative. Continuing in the same direction, the 'problem of order' – of how apparently separate and self-interested individuals can live together in a reasonably harmonious way – should not be seen as *the* central problem of sociology; order and conflict are both central.

The classical thinkers did produce two conflicting views of modern society, and Giddens uses these as an organising basis for his *Sociology: A Brief but Critical Introduction* (1982g). The first is the theory of industrial society, concerned primarily with the contrast between industrial and traditional societies. Capitalism is seen as only one type of industrial society, and the main focus is on the market and state intervention. In Durkheim, for example, class conflict is not the central mechanism of change, but something which will become regulated according to accepted norms, and classlessness is seen in terms of consumption rather than production. In Giddens's view, these problems belong to the nineteenth century and have now been superseded; in his later work, he focuses on the power of the state and military power as the important issues of the present day.

The second view was the Marxist one, which concentrated on capitalism and its supersession; Giddens seems to think that Marxism has not remained so caught up in the problems of the nineteenth century, not least because it has a conception of mechanisms of social change which can enable it to look at new developments. But as we shall see, he considers these conceptions themselves deficient. In *The Nation-State and Violence* (1985a), he argues that capitalism was a necessary precondition for the development of industrialism, but the two can exist separately. However, this is looking too far ahead. I want first to consider the three eggs that have gone bad.

THE BAD EGGS

Positivism

For present purposes, we can take positivism as a philosophy of science very close to the common-sense view of what the natural sciences do. Science investigates an external world and attempts, by means of theories and hypotheses, to explain what happens in that world. A good theory is one which can be tested against the world and proves to be true in the sense that it not only explains but also predicts what will happen. It does this by means of general laws, general causal statements such as all metals expand when heated. Sociological positivism assumes that there is no basic difference between social and natural sciences.

Giddens's view of positivism can perhaps be judged by the fact that the collection of readings he edited under the title of *Positivism and Sociology* (1974) consists entirely of extracts from the work of those opposed to the idea of a positivist social science. During the period of 'orthodox consensus', it was generally argued that either the social sciences were on principle like the natural sciences or that they were not. The latter position was usually argued on the basis that the social sciences are about human beings, who are qualitatively different from the objects studied by the natural sciences. Humans are reflective, thinking beings who can be aware of the knowledge produced about them and act accordingly. Atoms and molecules carry on in the same way whatever we know about them; this is not necessarily the case with people. Giddens firmly endorses this argument and emphasizes the importance of the social sciences as a force in social life, the very thing they study.

This means that social science cannot produce universal laws. Giddens goes beyond this to argue that the reflective ability of humans, the possibility of being able to do otherwise, means that we cannot easily make causal generalisations. 'Causes' in social science refers to people's reasons for doing things, and these reasons often involve social scientific knowledge. Causes are therefore, in social science, 'inherently unstable'. Any generalisation in social science is temporary, 'historical' in its nature.

If this is the case, then 'explanations' in social science are much closer to descriptions – descriptions of people's reasons for acting and, as we shall see, their intended and unintended consequences. Giddens was writing when positivism was coming under criticism even as a theory of natural science. The focus of these criticisms was the clear distinction that positivism draws between theory and observation, the former explaining the latter. The case is that no easy distinction can be made, and our observations are themselves 'theory-laden'. Our theory tells us, to some extent, what we actually see in the world. Such arguments are drawn on by Giddens and clearly fit in with the general thrust of his argument. In *Studies in Social and Political Theory* (1977), he adopts a suggestion from Quine (elaborated in Hesse 1979) that within a scientific theory, we cannot make a rigorous distinction between theoretical and observation terms; which is which can vary and is a matter of context and purpose. Any laws that exist in the theory are not universal laws but refer to a finite number of situations. Thus, as I understand it, 'all metals expand when heated' should be seen not as referring to every metal that has existed or might exist but, more reasonably, to all the metals we have seen so far. We posit it as a law, and there is a theory to explain it, but it is also and perhaps primarily an observation. Science consists of a network of such statements, the status of which is relative and variable. Giddens argues elsewhere, in *Central Problems in Social Theory* (1979a) that in the social sciences description and explanation are intimately connected, and that a description (of people's reasons, etc.) is an explanation if it enables us to answer a question about a situation.

A standard argument of positivism was that philosophical problems are distinct from scientific problems and that except in moments of crisis, philosophy does not enter into scientific work. Giddens argues that in fact philosophical issues are at the heart of social science, although in *The Constitution of Society* (1984), he wisely recognises that philosophical problems do not have to be *solved* before sociologists can learn from philosophy. In fact many of his new ingredients come from the philosopher's shop.

Functionalism

Functionalism, or perhaps more accurately structural-functionalism, was the dominant theory within sociology up until the mid-1960s. Giddens regards it as fundamentally positivist in its assumptions. Again a very general characterisation is all that is necessary here. It works with a notion of the whole – 'society' or 'systems' – being greater than the parts – 'individuals' or 'sub-systems' – and usually with an organic analogy. Society is like an organism and just as the different parts of the body are dependent upon each other and work to support each other, so the different parts of society depend upon and work for each other. Generally it includes an evolutionary view of history which can be understood through a similar organic analogy. Just as a cell divides and then divides again, each time forming a more complex structure, so society divides, developing more and more specialised institutions dealing with different aspects of life. Thus simple societies were primarily based on the kinship system; in modern society the family is just one specialist system amongst others: the economic system, the education system, the political system, etc. Explanations in terms of this theory are structural, in the sense that events and actions are determined by the requirements of the system to survive and remain stable.

Giddens's arguments against functionalism have much in common with his arguments against positivism: sociology is concerned with actors and actors' reasons for doing things. They seem to boil down to two points. Functionalism must adopt one of two positions, neither of which is tenable:

(1) one must presuppose that societies, social systems are actually agents, with needs and the ability to make decisions. I can only picture this by seeing society as a sort of Martian, an alien being with all the properties we attribute to people, only more so. In fact, I don't think anybody would pursue such a position seriously. Beyond this, there is the logical objection to functionalism: that even if societies have needs, the existence of a need does not mean that it will be met, or that it will be met in a particular way; or

(2) one must offer explanations which are in fact, as Cohen (1989) describes them, redundant, in the sense that they can always be redescribed in terms of the actors' knowledge of their world and reasons for doing things. The idea, for example, that the family in our society fulfils the function of early socialisation and thus contributes to maintaining the social system as a whole, can be redescribed in terms of the decisions, to act or not to act, of people who have children, who make up the government and civil service, the professional bodies concerned with socialisation, etc. These decisions, like all others, have a 'systematic' nature; this does not occur by accident, and most of Giddens's

theory is concerned to show how the systematic nature of human organisation comes about, without recourse to functionalist explanations.

He does rescue one idea from functionalism; if we drop the idea that functionalism actually explains anything, we can ask questions such as 'What would have to happen for the family to change in a certain way or remain the same?'. This presupposes in a fairly loose way ideas about the function of the family, but it provides a stimulus to imaginative thought and the formation of hypotheses which can then be translated into acceptable terms involving action and the consequences of action.

I will be discussing Giddens's arguments around functionalism at some length later, in particular looking at the modern resurgence of functionalism and its importance.

Evolutionary theories of history

Evolutionary theory shares with positivism and functionalism a conception of human life determined by social forces which exist over and above it – in this case, some more or less natural and inevitable movement from one form of society to another. Giddens is highly critical of evolutionary elements in Marxism and functionalism. In *The Constitution of Society* (1984), he identifies four dangers of evolutionary thought which he argues are best avoided by breaking radically with this way of thinking:

(1) *unilineal compression*: to regard one particular line of development as universal; the fact that feudalism precedes capitalism in Europe does not mean that this is the case everywhere;

(2) *homological compression*: the assumption of a parallel between individual development and social development; this is misleading because it assumes a comparative simplicity in early forms of society, and whilst this might be found in some areas, in others early societies were very complex;

(3) *normative illusion*: the assumption that societies higher on the evolutionary scale are in some way better because they have survived; all too often this simply amounts to saying that 'might is right'; and

(4) *temporal distortion*: as I understand it, the idea that the passage of time always involves change, evolution.

Giddens's main theoretical objection to evolutionary thought, however, is an objection to the idea that there is any one mechanism of social change, particularly that there is one mechanism within a society that pushes it forward along the evolutionary scale. In much functionalist thought, this mechanism is adaptation to the material environment. Giddens argues that in social theory, either the term is given such a general meaning that it includes everything that happens, and therefore becomes meaningless, or, when it is given a specific meaning, it is far too narrow to explain social change, or is clearly false, and/or it has all the logical deficiencies of functionalist explanations. The one evolutionary argument that would work, Giddens argues, is to attribute to human beings as such a particular goal, such as to improve their material environment, yet there is no evidence of such a goal.

The conception of social change that Giddens himself puts forward is, as we shall see later, that it follows no predetermined course and that it is the result of a number of factors, internal and external to a particular society, that come together at a particular time.

The one feature uniting all these rejections is that they see human action and human life as determined by forces outside of itself. Giddens's theory is, I shall argue, very much an action theory, what Giddens sometimes calls a theory of praxis, even in its analysis of structure.

THE NEW AND UNUSUAL INGREDIENTS

I now want to turn to the ingredients that Giddens does incorporate into his theoretical omelette. It is not a simple incorporation: the ingredients have to be peeled and processed first, and he draws his inspiration from so many sources that a full catalogue would be rather like rewriting his books. I am selecting simply the main ingredients: linguistic philosophy, phenomenological sociology and ethnomethodology, Goffman, psychoanalysis, hermeneutics, structuralism and post-structuralism, Marxism, Heidegger, and time–geography. In the case of structuralism and Marxism, much of the original is shed – it is less the core than perhaps the peel that is included; in the other cases, concepts and ideas are incorporated with comparatively little modification, but significant parts of the original are left behind.

Giddens sometimes presents his work as being rather more of a radical break with conventional sociology than it actually is. He states, for example, that sociology had no theory of action and that it was necessary in particular to take note of the 'linguistic turn' in modern philosophy. Of course a large part of classical and modern sociology has been concerned with the theory of action, even if the available theories were not satisfactory, and the discipline had, for a number of years before Giddens's first theoretical work, *New Rules of Sociological Method* (1976), been concerning itself with the 'linguistic turn'. Giddens's contribution was to bring many strands together and to give respectability to those sociologists who had been working in these areas.

By the *linguistic turn* Giddens means twentieth-century philosophy's increasing concern with language. For some, language has become the central model for all other human activities. It has become common to see the world around us and ourselves as somehow 'constituted' in and by language. There are good sociological reasons for this that I shall look at later. Giddens's attitude has modified over the years from the insistence that this approach should be registered by and become part of sociology to arguing that sociology should not fall into the trap of following it through to its logical conclusion: that there is a real world of social practices that are not simply constituted in language. It is beyond doubt, however, that the linguistic turn has left its mark on Giddens's social theory.

Linguistic philosophy

Under this heading, I include the work of Wittgenstein and various traditions of interpretation well established in English-speaking philosophy. For Giddens, perhaps the most important work in this tradition is Peter Winch's *The Idea of a Social Science* (1958). Winch's argument makes the assumption I mentioned above: that in a very real sense, our language *is* our world; and in particular, we cannot conceive of social relations apart from how people think and talk about them. The task of the sociologist is to elaborate the 'form of life' of a particular culture, the way in which it conceives of itself. Social action, according to Winch, is like language use, it is 'rule-following'. There is no satisfactory dictionary definition of the words we use

- they can be employed in a range of contexts. Football, for example, is a 'game', but my occupation can be the 'sociology game' and my lover can play 'games' with me – sexual 'games' or emotional 'games'. Although we cannot find a definition of the word which will cover all its uses, we can tell when a particular use is appropriate or inappropriate because there are socially agreed (but not necessarily conscious or explicit) rules governing the use of the word. In a similar way, our social action is rule-governed, and to elaborate on a culture is to elaborate on the rules which govern social action in that culture. Winch's position is relativist: we cannot judge between cultures, only understand each one; for example, we can understand what a certain society might mean by witchcraft, how it identifies witches and what witches do, and we can understand what our own society means by science, and what scientists do, but we cannot say that one is better than another. They are simply two different forms of life, two ways of living, of seeing the world.

Giddens criticises Winch on a number of grounds in *New Rules of Sociological Method* (1976), not least rejecting his relativism and his lack of concern with the reproduction of action, but the idea of action as rule-following becomes central to his notion of practices and structure.

Phenomenological sociology and ethnomethodology

During the 1960s, those trying to develop a sociological theory of action turned to European philosophy, in particular Husserl's phenomenology. Alfred Schutz, a pupil of Husserl, had concerned himself particularly with the extension of phenomenology to look at the social world. In particular, he developed a conception of common-sense, taken-for-granted knowledge which we build up through experience and on which we base our actions. Such an idea is important for Giddens, but he goes further, taking up a radical version presented in Harold Garfinkel's *Studies in Ethnomethodology* (1967), an approach so different from what had gone before that it was the subject of often bitter political battles in sociology departments.

Ethnomethodology attempted to transform the object of sociology away from social structures and systems, which were seen not as real things but conceptions produced by people, to the conversational properties of interaction, where such concepts are produced. Social structure, social order, is not something which exists out there in the world but is a constant product of our activities, primarily of talk. When we talk, we 'make sense' of or create a stable, ordered world where we feel secure. We do this by giving rational accounts of our actions which can be accepted by ourselves and others. In giving these rational accounts we use a range of resources and methods that are taken for granted – we do not think about them and are not usually conscious of them. They are none the less responsible for the stable and ordered world that we feel we live in. This world is something we create and re-create all the time, and it was common to attach the word 'doing' to activities which we would normally take for granted. In writing this book, for example, I am 'doing' being a sociologist, employing a range of techniques which establish that I am a sociologist engaging in sociological work.

Garfinkel's early work consisted of using his students to create situations in which this taken-for-granted knowledge was challenged. They would go into a shop and try to barter for goods, or behave like lodgers in their parents' homes, or carry on a conversation by constantly asking what the other person meant. This last is important because it shows what I mentioned in my discussion of Winch: that we cannot give any adequate meaning to our words – we can never actually say what we mean. Rather our continued interaction rests upon taken-for-granted techniques and rules to convey the impression of meaning. When these techniques and rules are not followed, disorder, confusion and anger result. It is as if I were to write this book backwards, in verse form; or leave out the verbs.

Now Giddens clearly wants to maintain some notion of structure and system, so ethnomethodology also has to be processed before it will suit the omelette. What Giddens takes and develops from this source is:

(1) the notion of reflexivity: that in giving a rational account of our actions we are actually constituting them and the social world in which we live. He generally gives it a wider meaning than the ethnomethodologists who confine its use to the ordering of conversation. For Giddens, it becomes our ability to reflect constantly on what we are doing, incorporate knowledge of ourselves and our situation and change our activities accordingly; and

(2) the notion of taken-for-granted or *implicit* knowledge; Giddens distinguishes between 'knowledge of what' and 'knowledge of how', the latter being usually implicit, taken for granted. He employs this idea to insist on the *knowledgeability* of human actors, their often implicit knowledge of how everything works; and he often quotes Garfinkel's comments to the effect that people are not structural or cultural 'dupes', acting in ways determined from the outside. We know what we are doing even if we cannot say what it is.

Goffman

The first thing that comes to mind for most sociologists when the name Goffman is mentioned is the apparent individual 'quirkiness' of his work; it is as if only Goffman could do it. He sees the small detail of people's interactions and takes apart the ways in which we present ourselves in the most everyday situations. It is odd to find him incorporated into 'grand theory', yet Giddens devotes much space to him in *The Constitution of Society* (1984), and there is an essay on 'Erving Goffman as a Systematic Social Theorist' in *Social Theory and Modern Sociology* (1987a).

I think that Giddens is quite right to treat Goffman in this way, and his interests in the routine nature of social action and interaction lead him to this interpretation. One of Goffman's concerns is the way in which we work with each other to maintain the flow and propriety of our everyday interaction, to make sure that it runs smoothly, and we all give good performances. He is concerned with what Giddens calls *tact*. He is also concerned with what, using his own 'dramaturgical' metaphor, we might call stage management, the ways in which we organise the space around us in our self-presentation and ensure that one thing follows another as it should: entrances and exits run smoothly, people take turns at talking when appropriate and so on. Another way of putting this is that Goffman is interested in the formal properties of social interaction, not the specific content of each occasion, but the way in which we organise occasions themselves. In Goffman's own terms, it is 'frame analysis' – the concern is not with the picture itself but with what surrounds it. Like Garfinkel, he is concerned with taken-for-granted knowledge of how to act, but in such a way that, as we shall see later, Giddens can use him to link the analysis of social systems with social action.

Psychoanalysis

Giddens seems always to have had a slightly more than passing interest in psychoanalysis. In a very early paper, 'A Typology of Suicide' (1966), he distinguishes between different forms of suicide and suicide attempts by employing psychoanalytic concepts to investigate the different meanings of suicide. In structuration theory, he draws on psychoanalysis on a number of occasions, usually and interestingly when he wants to underline the importance of *routine* in our daily lives, which he connects to what he calls ontological security, a sense of 'safeness', of really being in and part of the world, which is in turn a necessary aspect of the working of social systems. When he considers the breakdown of routine, crisis situations, he employs Freud's crowd psychology and talks of regression to infantile stages of development and identification with a leader–figure in an attempt to regain the lost security.

Giddens's most important borrowing from the point of view of what I want to argue later is from the work of Erik Erikson and object-relations theory. Erikson's work is wide ranging and notable for its concern with the internal dynamic aspects of the individual's existence but also for how he considers the external forms of social organisation and the ways in which the two interrelate and interlock. He belongs to the major American school of psychoanalysis, generally known as 'ego-psychology', and is concerned centrally with the ways in which people adjust to their environment. One of Erikson's most famous papers, in *Childhood and Society* (Erikson 1977), dealt with what he sees as the eight stages of psycho-social development; Giddens's borrowing is from his analysis of the first stages. Each stage is seen in terms of an opposition of positive and negative personality qualities, a successful resolution leaving one placed more towards the positive than the negative end of the continuum.

The first stage is a fundamental one in which the infant learns, or fails to learn, a basic trust in the world. A basic trust comes from the reliability of nursing, good feeding, warmth - especially the warmth of physical presence - and relationship. In *The Constitution of Society* (1984), Giddens links this with the development of ontological security, and emphasises especially the routine nature of good nursing and caring, through which the baby grasps that he/she is the same person at different times and different places.

Hermeneutics

Hermeneutics is the science of interpretation, concerned with what it is to understand something, to find meaning in it. It is an analysis – going back to Winch – of forms of life, traditions of thinking, perhaps more concerned with explicit than implicit meaning and the rules of different discourses. Giddens comes to hermeneutics via a debate between the leading German hermeneutic thinker, Hans-Georg Gadamer, and the modern representative of critical theory, Jurgen Habermas. Giddens sees himself as arguing for a 'hermeneutically informed social theory'; a paper in *Studies in Social and Political Theory* (1977) tries to bring together several of these traditions. In a sense they are all about what it means to understand, and by the time of writing *The Constitution of Society* (1984), Giddens tends to treat 'hermeneutic' as a general term for the issues I have mentioned so far. Generally hermeneutics is criticised for being unable to account for what Giddens calls the unacknowledged conditions and consequences of human action – there are limits to the knowledgeability of social actors.

Giddens places much emphasis on what he calls the 'double hermeneutic', which he sees as a vital aspect of social theory and sociology. The idea is drawn from all the above approaches and rests upon the realisation that sociology, and the concepts it employs, are related intimately to the ideas and concepts of the non-sociologist. The construction and mastery of a theory is itself a hermeneutic task, a form of 'practical activity' that must take its place alongside other forms of activity, like mastering a language or a skill; but at the same time it is interpreting into its own framework others which are already established and employed in the social world. There is a constant 'slippage' between the discourse of sociology and the discourses of its object, of social life; and this is a two-way process. It is because positivism cannot grasp this double hermeneutic that it has to be rejected.

Structuralism and post-structuralism

On the face of it, structuralism should come in for the same rejection as structural-functionalism. At the peak of its fashion, adherents were announcing the 'death of the subject'; the human actor was seen as a product of structures, not as a producer, as an individual making choices and decisions and acting of his or her 'own free will'. However, except for its Marxist variant, the structures under consideration were not external to the individual, acting from the outside, but internal. The first structuralist discipline was linguistics – more specifically the linguistics of Saussure.

Saussure (1960) made a number of important distinctions that were later to be incorporated into several other disciplines: anthropology, the history of ideas, philosophy, sociology, psychoanalysis and the study of a range of cultural phenomena. The distinction that is important for what I have to say here is that between *speech* and *language*. Speech is, obviously, what we say. Our speech acts are unique, varying from context to context, and they cannot become the object of a science. The language is a structure out of which our speech acts are produced (or, as later structuralists would say, which produce our speech acts). A language can be analysed as a set of conventional signs which draw their meaning from their relationship to each other, not because of any necessary link between the word and its object. Thus the meaning of *table* emerges not from any necessary connection between the word and this wooden object in front of me, but because calling it a table distinguishes it from a chair, a wall, a bookcase or whatever, and these signs are agreed upon by those of us who speak the same language. At its most basic level, a language is a structure of signs and rules governing the way in which the signs can be combined together.

It should be clear by now that structuralism is very much part of the linguistic turn of modern thought, and it is not surprising that when Giddens develops his conception of structure, he employs, at least by analogy, something very much like the structuralist conception. He is very critical of structuralism when he discusses it directly in *Central Problems in Social Theory* (1979a), for reasons one might expect. These can be classed as broadly 'realist' – Saussure is criticised for removing any possibility of understanding the referential nature of language and for losing what Giddens considers the essential relation between meaning and practice. When he discusses the work of Levi-Strauss, who sees himself as talking about basic structures of the mind, Giddens sees the same gap between the structure and practical, conscious activities, to the detriment of the latter. The subject of action, the actor, is eliminated.

Yet at the same time as he makes these criticisms, Giddens employs notions of structural analysis such as the distinction between syntagmatic and paradigmatic levels (the meaning of which need not concern us here) and he employs ideas from structuralism to introduce the importance of time and space to his own theory. These ideas are, I think, best understood when we look at other sources, and I am not sure that it is right to say that he incorporates these ideas from structuralism; rather he uses structuralism as an analogy and a prompt. I think the important element he takes is the notion of structure itself as an underlying framework of elements and rules from which practices are produced by conscious actors. One topic of frequent criticism in his theory is the ontological status he gives to 'structures' – when and how they exist. Their existence seems to me to have the same peculiarities as the existence of the structure of language, or the structures of thought.

Post-structuralism is in many ways more radical than structuralism, and even more difficult to characterise briefly. It is equally firm in its rejection of classical notions viewing the subject as a simple origin of actions, maker of decisions and so on. It is, in my opinion, very much a product of the modern world and the difficulties that we experience trying to live within it. The emphasis is not so much on the difficulty of making sense of our lives, of finding meaning, but on the absence of meaning. The self is seen in its nature as divided and/or fragmented, and the idea of underlying structures disappears: instead there is the constant play of language and meaning. Giddens seems to find this interesting, and in *Central Problems in Social Theory* (1979a) his discussion of Derrida and Kristeva is rather sympathetic. These two are more concerned with the processes involved in structuring, or, if you like, constituting the supposedly active subject. Here his main criticism again is that these processes by which we are created as subjects are inherently connected to a much wider range of social practices which the post-structuralists ignore. And although Giddens accepts that the social actor is 'constructed' (more conventional thinkers talk about socialisation), he argues that the end product, the self-conscious social actor, is still important if not central.

Nevertheless, Giddens takes a number of ideas from poststructuralist thinkers. He emphasises the play of presence and absence in Derrida's philosophy, connecting it to the idea that the presence of one element in a structure implies others that are absent. He also uses Lacan's structural psychoanalysis to discuss the development of the self or actor. Most important, though, in the development of his theoretical work and his historical sociology, is his borrowing from Foucault.

As with those from other philosophical thinkers discussed in this chapter, this borrowing is specific and does not take on the philosophical baggage that could go with it. Amongst other things, Foucault is interested in the relationship between power and knowledge and takes up a theme found in Nietzsche that reverses the common-sense way of thinking about the two that is prevalent in liberal and socialist societies. Usually we think of knowledge as a liberation; it enables us to do things. It can, however, also be thought of as power and oppression. The development of professions such as medicine, based on modern scientific knowledge, can be seen as the development of the power of modern society to organise and control our bodies. In *Discipline and Punish* (1979), Foucault is concerned with the development of modern penal systems away from punishing the body to disciplining and organising it, and in this connection, with the importance of surveillance. For Giddens, the modern state is distinguished by its immense powers of surveillance of everyday activities, and Foucault has hit upon something very important.

Marxism

In one of his latest essays (in Held and Thompson 1989), Giddens says that there is much more to Marxism that he would reject than he would accept. It seems to me that like most non-Marxist sociologists, he has had a rather strange and ambivalent relationship to Marxism. It often seems as if the ghost of Marx stands behind any theorist concerned with the nature of modern society, influencing ideas against the will of the theorist, constantly throwing spanners into the works. It was not until he was well into the development of his own theory that Giddens felt able to confront Marxism in a systematic way. His objections can be predicted from what has gone before: he is critical of the evolutionary aspect of Marxism, the idea that society moves through determinate stages; of structural versions of Marxism that see the individual as simply the 'bearer' of underlying relations; and of the 'class reductionism' and/or 'economic reductionism' of Marxism that sees everything in terms of the struggle between collective entities or the contradiction between the forces and relations of production.

What Giddens takes from Marx, he argues, is first the full weight of Marx's statement that people make history, but not in circumstances of their own choosing – what Giddens refers to in other places as the unacknowledged conditions and consequences of action. As with some of the ideas that he elaborates on from his critique of structuralism, one does not actually need the origins to hold onto the outcome. There are, however, notions from Marx's analysis of capitalism that Giddens does incorporate into his theory, and this is the second debt that he acknowledges. Conceptually, it seems to me, his notions of contradiction and structural sets owe much to Marx, as do his more empirical analyses of capitalism. In *A Contemporary Critique of Historical Materialism* (1981a), he argues that his most important disagreement with Marx lies in his (Giddens's) emphasis on 'the search for meaning' in human life.

Beyond this, there is Giddens's rather complicated relationship to critical theory and the Frankfurt School, in particular to Jurgen Habermas, its most important contemporary representative. Most of Giddens's work on Habermas is highly critical, and it is common to hear these two mentioned in the same breath as modern representatives of grand theory and, by implication, competitors. Habermas is certainly systematic in a way that Giddens is not, and many of the latter's criticisms have to do with the failure of the system. However, he makes much of his concern to identify and develop the critical potential of sociology and modern social theory, which he sees as inherent in their nature. I will be devoting some time to these issues later on.

Heidegger

Martin Heidegger was a German philosopher who is usually classed as an 'existentialist'; his most important work was published through the first half of this century, and his work and career are controversial through his association with the Nazi party in Hitler's Germany. Heidegger employed the phenomenological method of Husserl to investigate those questions that the non-philosopher perhaps takes to be the meat and drink of philosophy: the nature of our existence and the meaning of our lives and of our relationship to the world around us. The solid objects amongst which we live, our ideas and our scientific knowledge, are seen as secondary constructs, sometimes as things we produce for ourselves to hide from our real and unavoidable situation, which is perhaps too painful for us to bear. This investigation of the world of experience that lies behind knowledge, of 'human being', *dasein*, is an investigation of the ontological, the nature of being itself; normal scientific investigation concerns the 'ontic', the things we produce out of our world of primordial experience.

In particular, our measurable time is external to us and hides our real existence, less *in* time but *as* time. Time is a vital aspect of our existence, one of our defining characteristics: we *are* temporal beings; time is constitutive of our human being. The past and the future are as real and important to us as the present, and Heidegger talks of us 'presencing' ourselves. The immediate situation around us, what is at hand to us, is – at the most basic level of analysis – our world. Part of human suffering comes from the fact that our future holds our death and that we are alone in the face of death, and, for Heidegger, the 'authentic' character involves a recognition of this and a caring about it.

As in other cases, Giddens takes much of importance from Heidegger, and after a while the mention of Heidegger tends to fade from his writings. Most important, and setting the tone for much of his later work, he takes the idea of the constitutive nature of time and space and the distinction between time at the ontological level and our measurable 'ontic' time; time and space then become ways of analysing and comparing societies, through the different ways in which they combine or 'bind' time and space. The second central idea that he takes is of the existential contradiction between our apparent immortality as symbolic beings – our words and ideas can, it seems, last for ever – and our finite physical existence: we are, each of us, going to die. This, he argues, is translated into social contradictions.

Time-geography

Giddens's insistence on the importance of time and space led naturally, it seems, to an encounter with modern time-geography, associated most closely with the name of Hagerstrand (1975 and 1976). Time-geography has developed ways of tracing patterns and constructing models of people's movements through time and space and offers Giddens a way of 'mapping' social systems, although as a good sociologist should, he insists that time-geography has neglected the structural aspects of this patterning. Nevertheless, this treatment of 'ontic' time plays a central role in his description of social systems.

Conclusion

In writing this chapter, I have occasionally felt I was getting lost, the point was disappearing, and I imagine the same experience might occur when reading it. If that is the case, then I have reproduced an effect of reading Giddens himself. He moves around from topic to topic, point to point, thinker to thinker, and I find myself struggling to find the 'point'. It is rather like trying to read an omelette. I have none the less pursued this tactic for two reasons. The first is to emphasise my omelette analogy: Giddens is cracking open philosophers and mixing their contents together, and then adding other ingredients, the theoretical equivalents of cheese and mushrooms and onions, etc. I do not object to this way of working as such; it is, in fact, the way we all work if we read widely in and outside our fields. Rather what I will argue, when I come to work through my criticisms of structuration theory, is that what is rejected when he processes his ingredients is of considerable importance. He peels his mushrooms when the peel is the most nutritional part. The second is to give some idea of the sheer scope of Giddens's reading and thinking, which would, I think, daunt any other working sociologist.

The 'point' of it all is that there are clear focuses of attention in all this. There is the dominant concern with theories of social action, language and implicit knowledge; with a particular conception of structure and system, and with time and space as dimensions of analysis; and there is Giddens's continuous debate with Marxism.

In the next chapter, I will move on to an outline of structuration theory itself. Here I will drop the omelette analogy - it is, in the end, impossible to read or to write an omelette. Instead I will return to an analogy I used in the introduction: Giddens's Lego, sets of theoretical building bricks that slot into each other in a variety of ways and can be fitted together to build a range of different models. This analogy catches the other side of his work, his more systematic and synthetic intent.

Chapter 3

Structuration theory

THE CENTRE OF THE THEORY

This chapter, too, is likely to suffer the same difficulty as the last: that of losing the reader (not to mention the writer) as we move through the different sections of Giddens's theory. It is worth repeating that it is not, nor does Giddens claim or want it to be, a tight, logically deduced and interrelated theory. This makes exposition difficult: it could – almost – be set out in any order, and the order I am choosing has much to do with the line of criticism I want to develop later. In what follows, I will do my best to provide retrospective and prospective links. My method of setting out the theory is a compromise between following its development in Giddens's own work and trying to provide an analytic coherence in which the ideas gain some logical connection with each other, even if it is one imposed by myself rather than Giddens.

The difficulty in getting hold of Giddens's theory as a whole is perhaps indicated by the nature of the critiques so far published: three out of four are collections of papers dealing with different and partial aspects of his work. Richard Bernstein (in Held and Thompson 1989) quotes William James to the effect that 'any author is easy if you catch the centre of his vision', and he rightly identifies the notion of the duality of structure as the centre of Giddens's work. Bernstein argues that the swing between concern with the individual agent and structural patterns is typical of the human sciences in general, not just sociology, and Giddens's attempt to overcome this and to reconstruct social theory is entirely praiseworthy.

What Giddens means by the duality of structure can be put in various ways. A conventional way of looking at 'structure' in sociology is to see it as something which constrains action, or even determines it; Giddens argues that it is also enabling, it makes it possible for us to do things. This seems to me to be self-evident: if we use the analogy with language, then it is clear that the language we use prohibits us from saying some things, but it equally clearly enables us to say something. Similarly, sociological theories of action have perhaps assumed that there were no constraints on action when, equally clearly, there are.

We cannot say that structure and action are the same thing, but neither can we give any absolute priority to one or the other. Giddens's solution to this is to argue that we should be concerned with social practices, as he does in the passage I cited in the first chapter (Giddens 1984; see p. 3). It is social practices which constitute (or socialise) us as actors, and which also embody or realise structures. Thus, though structure and action are not the same thing, they are not different things either; rather they are two aspects of, corresponding to different ways of looking at, the same thing: social practices. Thus we can look at any social situation or phenomenon from the point of view of 'strategic action' or from that of 'institutional analysis', and employ, in Giddens's approach, sets of compatible concepts (as opposed to mutually exclusive concepts) for so doing. This concentration on social practices enables Giddens to present himself as a theorist of praxis – a term used frequently, but not only, in Marxist theory, and emphasising the creative and transformative aspects of action – and to claim to have brought a new and necessary coherence to sociological theory.

The 'duality of structure' is, if you like, the 'secret formula' which is employed in producing the components of Giddens's Lego.

ACTION AND THE ACTOR
Action

I am beginning with Giddens's conception of action and the actor, partly because that is where he himself begins, in *New Rules of Sociological Method* (1976), and partly because I believe it is essential to understand this before his conception of structure becomes intelligible and the rest of his conceptual framework unfolds.

The centrality of action to structuration theory, at least in its early stages, is enshrined in Giddens's first two rules:

'A.1. Sociology is not concerned with a 'pre-given' universe of objects but with one which is constituted or produced by the active doings of subjects.

A.2. The production and reproduction of society thus has to be treated as a skilled performance on the part of its members.
(Giddens 1976: 160)

In this sense, action, or agency, is the centre of sociological concern. The crucial feature of action is that it is not determined; here the importance of Winch's conception of action as rule-following becomes clear, since there is always more than one way of following a rule, a right way and a wrong way. When we talk of action, an implication is that it is always possible to have acted otherwise. Giddens goes on to make a clear distinction between what he describes as 'event-causality' and 'agent-causality'; the former involves regular, invariant relations between cause and effect, whilst the latter involves 'necessary connections' and an idea of causal efficacy. As I understand it, 'necessary connections' means that the relationship between my 'reflexive monitoring' of what I am doing and the action I undertake is a sufficient explanation of my action. I don't have to act in the same way on other occasions.

Arguing against linguistic philosophy, Giddens claims action is a continuous flow, a process which can't be broken down into reasons, motives, intentions, etc. to be treated as separate entities. Rather it is a process which we constantly monitor and 'rationalise'. My action is rooted in my knowledge of myself and the world, and rationalisation is the 'causal expression' of that. Reflexivity, Giddens often claims, is a distinguishing and vital feature of human action. *Verstehen* – the process of understanding – is not, as it was for Weber, simply a method: it is *the* ontological condition of human society.

A feature of action which has considerable significance for Giddens is its transformative power; at times, as Archer (1982) notes, he writes as if action is always creative, transformative. He builds a central aspect of his theory, the analysis of power, on this. Power becomes an inherent and necessary feature of human relationships since it is inherent in the definition of action itself –

the ability to do or achieve or change something. This provides
the basis of his arguments against functionalist conceptions of
power, where it is seen as a system product, and against Marxist
conceptions, where it seen as connected with certain forms of
property rights. Because it is inherent in human action, power
can never be absolute, nor can it disappear. Action is not only
transformative, however; it also has normative and commu-
nicative dimensions which are basic to it. These stem from the
fact that action involves rules and rule-following, and that all
action is social, since it implicates rules.

Giddens argues that unintended consequences are as much the
result of action as intended consequences, since they would not
occur if the action did not take place. One of his arguments
against functionalism emerges here. For Merton (1968),
'unintended consequences' are seen not as a result of action, but
as a result of the functional workings of the social system. Thus
one of the unintended consequences of my writing this book is
that the washing up doesn't get done, and after a while my wife
steps in and does it. For a functionalist, this would be seen in
terms of the way in which the family system allocates different
roles to its members, so that they complement each other and
keep the system going. For Giddens, it makes no sense to talk of
the system doing anything; I do something and my action
produces a series of intended and unintended consequences, in
reaction to which other people choose to act or not to act.

Giddens's conception of action has certain existentialist affinities: the ability to act is prior to our reflexive ability – it is always
there and we must act; we are, perhaps, doomed to act. Giddens
does not choose to follow this line of thought, instead emphasising the central importance of reflexivity, freedom – the ability to
do otherwise – its nature as a process, and its transformative
capacity.

The transformative capacity of action is, as I. Cohen (1989)
puts it, 'utilised' in social practices, but before we can talk about
social practices, it is necessary to look not only at agents but at
structures, the nature of time and space and so on, eventually
coming back to interaction. Action is a sort of base for the Lego,
its features becoming hidden as various pieces are added to it and
different models built up.

This leads on to the issue of the relationship between action, or
agency, and the actor or agent. Again I. Cohen (1989) offers a

useful formulation: Giddens gives priority to the making of history rather than the makers; in this sense he can be seen as taking up the structuralist and post-structuralist theme of 'decentering' the subject, and we could almost talk about the actor as constituted in and by practices. To a certain extent, this is how Giddens does see the actor, but the actor is not an epiphenomenon – people remain very much at the centre of his theory. They are not, however, pure originators of action nor are they simple products of socialisation.

The actor

Action by itself, of course, is not sufficient. If that is the base of the Lego, there are a number of pieces which, when put together, make up 'actors' or 'agents'. I mentioned earlier that Giddens criticises modern philosophies of action for not taking, or for being unable to take, account of the unacknowledged conditions of action and of the unintended consequences of action. One of the conditions or limitations on action is the actor's body and physical capabilities. However, there is rather more to it than this. In the course of his work, Giddens develops what he calls a 'stratified' conception of the actor, or agent. There are, he argues, three levels involved, and he draws a rough analogy to Freud's structural model of the psyche: id, ego and super-ego, although he acknowledges that his three levels are not equivalent. Perhaps the closest connection is between the id and Giddens's 'unconscious', the level of motivation; to this, he adds the level of the rationalisation of action, and that of the reflexive monitoring of action: 'practical consciousness' and 'discursive consciousness' respectively.

Motivation, the unconscious

The level of motivation is unconscious, and also, for Giddens, the most divorced from action itself. He is critical of any Freudian attempt to reduce consciousness to the result of the activity of subterranean 'dark forces'. For Giddens, dark forces only become important at exceptional moments when the fabric of everyday life is threatened or broken.

Motives are seen as the actor's 'wants', and they refer to potential for action rather than action itself. Unlike Freud,

Motives are
not wishes

Giddens does not see people as driven by their 'wants': because I have various 'wants', it does not follow that I necessarily have to act on them, except in exceptional circumstances. However, Giddens does see them as having a generalised influence on action, providing overall plans or programmes for action.

Reflexivity

Practical consciousness

Here Giddens draws directly from ethnomethodology and phenomenological sociology. He constantly emphasises the knowledgeability of actors, arguing that it simply isn't true that institutions or society work behind people's backs. Yet our knowledge of what is going on is not always explicit and it is not always easy to make it explicit; nevertheless we know what we are doing, or, perhaps more accurately, we know how to do it. We are conscious of these things in a practical, taken-for-granted way, we routinely 'rationalise' what we do.

Discursive consciousness

Discursive consciousness is our ability to reflect upon our actions and describe, monitor and give rational accounts of them. There is no clear dividing line between discursive and practical consciousness, but a constant movement between the two. We can often, if asked, give a rational account of what we are doing, but we do not bear that account in mind all the time. The more fundamental or basic our activity, the more difficult it often is to provide that account.

There is one more very important quality that Giddens attributes to the actor: ontological security, a sense of safety, that I mentioned in the last chapter. In *The Constitution of Society* (1984), it is defined as 'Confidence and trust that the natural and social worlds are as they appear to be, including the basic existential parameters of self and social identity' (Giddens 1984: 375).

The term 'trust' becomes more central in Giddens's more recent work, as he develops the ideas of Erik Erikson. Throughout he emphasises the importance of *routine* as a source of security, and as I mentioned earlier, he sees Garfinkel's early experiments as representing the breaking of routine and therefore representing a threat to or damaging ontological security. This explains the frequently angry reaction of the victims of these experiments. At different times he draws on different writers to explain the development of ontological security, but given his concern with consciousness, be it practical or discursive, and his emphasis on the knowledgeability of the actor, it is not surprising that he finds ego psychology more attractive than those forms of psychoanalysis that emphasise the powerful and disruptive role of the unconscious.

I will go into Giddens's discussions of Erikson's stages in a little more detail. As I pointed out earlier, in the first stage the development of trust depends upon the continuity of care and the introjection of a sense of being cared for; clearly routine plays an important part in this, and enables the child to realise that the absence of the mother does not mean that he or she has been deserted: the mother will routinely return, and in her absence, the infant can 'carry' her presence in his or her head. Giddens emphasises routine and the development of mechanisms to deal with tension. He also describes this development in the child as the ability to 'bind time and space', an idea to which I will return later.

The second stage, that during which the infant develops, to different degrees, a sense of autonomy or shame, Giddens links to his treatment of Goffman. Maintaining a sense of ontological security depends on a successful negotiation of the first stage but also the continuation of routine in major parts of one's life. One of the ways in which we deal with the everyday tensions that threaten our security is by a mutual tact which enables us to 'keep face' in our everyday interactions – to avoid, as it were, 'showing our behinds' (this stage is equivalent to Freud's anal stage). Goffman's work is concerned with, amongst other things, the division of our personal areas into front and back spaces; in the first, we perform our social roles; in the second we relax from them. Giddens seems to be claiming that the ability to achieve these performances is learnt through this second stage of development; we have already developed a trust in the world which enables us to employ and to expect from others the tactful behaviour which maintains our security, our 'face'.

The idea of the actor's sense of ontological security, based on routine, plays an important role in Giddens's theory. I will argue later that it is of more fundamental importance than he himself acknowledges. He uses it to gain a purchase on the experience of the modern world, where, he argues, routine, morally sanctioned by tradition, begins to break down and ontological security becomes more problematic. In *Central Problems in Social Theory* (1979a), he uses the analysis of what he calls 'critical situations' to emphasise the importance of routine, drawing on the work of, amongst others, Bettelheim on concentration camps to show that when routine breaks down there is a 'regression' to earlier stages of development, and in particular a tendency to deal with the resulting insecurity by a childlike identification with a leader, mirroring the original mother–child identification. This type of analysis later becomes the means by which he approaches the phenomenon of nationalism.

The actor, then, can be seen in terms of three levels: the unconscious, practical consciousness, and reflexive, discursive consciousness. The last two are more important than the first because an essential feature of the actor is his or her knowledgeability or awareness of the social context in which he or she is situated. The actor also gains through socialisation, and the routines of daily life, a sense of ontological security, safety in the world. However, it is important to bear in mind as well the existential contradiction which, although Giddens argues is alleviated as we move away from tribal societies, still remains in the background.

To understand routines and knowledgeability further, we need to look at Giddens's conception of structure. This takes us to a set of even more complex pieces of Lego; we already have the base and a set of pieces out of which we can construct actors; 'structures' enable us to bring these actors into a variety of relationships with each other.

STRUCTURES AND STRUCTURATION

It is easiest to begin by saying what Giddens does not mean by 'structures'. First, they do not have an existence external to the actor or to action. Giddens equates such a view, which he attributes to structural-functionalism and, in some respects, perhaps to structuralism itself and to some forms of Marxism, with determinism, and that is already excluded in the conception of action with which he starts. Secondly, they are *not* patterns or systems of interaction: this is the sense also sometimes attributed to structure by structural-functionalism. Giddens believes that the concept of system is important, but argues that systems *have* structures or at least 'structural properties'; they are not themselves structures.

We cannot abandon the idea of structure. Society, social interaction, is clearly 'structured' in some sense or another. It is not a process of pure, *ad hoc* creation; there are features of social life that are more or less widespread and that endure for a shorter or longer time and these cannot be explained in terms of the inherent properties of action. But if structures do not exist in a way that might be empirically observed, externally, or as social systems, then how do they exist? Giddens's answer, from *New Rules of Sociological Method* (1976) onwards, employs a linguistic analogy. He often makes it clear that he is not saying that 'society is like a language', and in his later work he separates himself from the linguistic turn in modern philosophy, but the analogy with language does seem to me to be central to his thought; society might not be like a language, but the relationship between structure and action is like the relationship between language and speech.

I will move through the concept of structure, beginning with its most abstract aspects and moving forward to the most concrete.

The existence of structures

There is a quotation from *New Rules of Sociological Method* (1976) which makes clear Giddens's comparison of structure and language, combining his denial of using an analogy with the analogy itself:

> An approach to the analysis of structures in sociology can be made by comparing what I will now simply call 'speech' (action and interaction) with language (structure), the latter being an abstract 'property' of a community of speakers. This is not an *analogy*. I am definitely not claiming that 'society is like a language'. (a) Speech is 'situated', i.e. spatially and temporally located, whereas language is . . . 'virtual and outside of time'. (b) Speech presupposes a subject, whereas language is specifically subject-less – even if it does not 'exist' except in so far as it is 'known' to, and produced by, its speakers. (c) Speech always potentially acknowledges the presence of another. . . . (L)anguage as a structure, on the

other hand, is neither an intended product of any one subject, nor oriented towards another. In sum, generalising this, practices are the situated doings of a subject, can be examined with regard to intended outcomes, and may involve an orientation towards securing a response. . . . [S]tructures, on the other hand, have no specific socio-temporal location, are characterised by the 'absence of a subject', and cannot be framed in terms of a subject–object dialectic.

(Giddens 1976: 118-19)

Giddens often repeats the point that structures have a *virtual* existence, later referring to it as 'momentary'. In *Central Problems in Social Theory* (1979a), he adds that structures are not models of reality produced by the observer, any more than the structure of language is a model. The linguistic analogy remains important here. The structure of language only exists in and through speech acts, and can be analysed in terms of 'rules of transformation' which enable us to produce an apparently infinite number of speech acts from a finite number of sounds. Similarly, structures in social life are rules of transformation (and for Giddens all rules are rules of transformation) which are present only in the social action which, as he puts it, 'instantiates' the structure. And just as each speech act implies and draws upon the whole structure of the language, so each social action implies and draws upon the structure it instantiates. In the language of French structuralism, which influences Giddens considerably in this book, the structure is present in its absence. He does, however, give some indication of how this 'absent structure' is carried, or perhaps even of where it exists:

To regard structure as involving a 'virtual order' . . . implies recognising the existence of (a) knowledge – as memory traces – of 'how things are to be done' (said, written) on the part of social actors; (b) social practices organised through the recursive mobilisation of that knowledge; (c) capabilities that the production of these practices presuppose.

(Giddens 1979a: 64)

Thus, if structures have a locus of existence, it is in the head of social actors. In *The Constitution of Society* (1984), Giddens describes social practices not as having structures, but as exhibiting structural properties, and again makes the reference to memory traces (Giddens 1984: 17).

Giddens continues with his linguistic analogy in another way. In structural linguistics, and in structuralist theories in most disciplines, there is a distinction between syntagm and paradigm, or the syntagmatic level and the paradigmatic level. The language is analysed as a structure of signs and rules about the combination of signs. The paradigmatic level refers to rules about which signs may substitute for others, changing the meaning of the word – for example, if we take the words *cat, mat, bat, fat, hat,* the paradigmatic level can be expressed thus:

m
b
cat
f
h

The structure of significant signs, signs which cause a change in meaning when substituted for each other, has in Giddens's terms a virtual existence – it is not out there in time and space. We know the procedures, the rules that enable us to vary the meaning of words by substituting these significant elements for each other.

The syntagmatic level, on the other hand, consists of rules governing the combination of signs in succession to each other, in words; they are rather like the grammatical rules which govern the construction of sentences. For example, in English, g and *h* can follow each other whereas x and z may not. Combinations of signs in this sense can have an existence in time and space. For Giddens, if structures represent the paradigmatic level of analysis, then social systems, patterns of interaction and social relationships, represent the syntagmatic level. They do have an existence in time and space. The consistent and ordered nature of this existence is a result of structure; and Giddens argues that this enables us to understand the reproduction of action as well as action itself – something to which linguistic philosophy pays scant attention.

Structuration and the duality of structure

It makes sense at this point to look briefly at the idea of structuration itself. This is the notion that Giddens puts at the centre of his theory, and which enables him to give priority to

[handwritten margin notes: "priority to"; "soc practices"]

social practices as opposed to actors and structures. Structuration, as I understand it, goes on in social practices, and it is the process of the production, reproduction and transformation of structures. The 'duality of structure' refers to the fact that structures are both produced by human action and are what Giddens calls the *medium* of human action. In *New Rules of Sociological Method* (1976), he again uses the analogy with language:

> Language exists as a 'structure', syntactical and semantic, only insofar as there are some kind of traceable consistencies in what people say, in the speech acts which they perform. From this aspect, to refer to rules of *syntax*, for example, is to refer to the reproduction of 'like elements'; on the other hand, such rules also *generate* the totality of speech-acts which is the spoken language. It is this dual aspect of structure, as both inferred from observation of human doings, yet as also operating as a medium whereby those doings are made possible, that has to be grasped through the notions of structuration and reproduction.
>
> (Giddens 1976: 121-2)

From now on in this book the notion of structuration will recur regularly, as will that of the duality of structure, and I will not devote specific sections to them.

Rules

Structures are rules and resources, or, as Giddens sometimes puts it, generative rules and resources. In *Studies in Social and Political Theory* (1977), he elaborates on the nature of rules. Social action is not simply rule-following in Winch's sense, in the way that game-playing is rule-following: the application of a rule in social life involves differential access to resources, and the rules in social life are more subject to dispute than the rules of a game. Rules are embedded in systems of social interaction – structures do not exist separately from systems of interaction except, I suppose, in their 'virtual' sense. In *Central Problems in Social Theory* (1979a), he points out that rules are not general descriptions of existing practices and that it is important to distinguish between knowing a rule and knowing how to formulate a rule. It is often the case that we cannot formulate the rules that we follow, but this does not mean that we do not know them. We cannot always formulate the semantic rules we follow when we speak, but clearly we must know them – otherwise nobody would understand us. Importantly, Giddens argues that one of the lessons of ethnomethodology has been that there is often *no* clear lexical formulation of a rule possible. There is always what Garfinkel calls an 'etcetera clause' at work in our interpretation of rules which enables us to vary our interpretation according to whatever circumstances we find ourselves in (Garfinkel 1967). Such a clause, Giddens argues, is inherent in the rules themselves.

In *The Constitution of Society* (1984), Giddens embarks on another discussion of the nature of rules, this time presumably fuelled by a number of criticisms of his work. In social life, he argues, rules always come in sets; they are not singular and applicable to single items of conduct, and they have two aspects to them: on the one hand, they relate to the constitution of meaning and on the other, to the sanctioning of conduct. He makes the notion of the duality of structure a little clearer in the discussion, in the sense that he goes beyond talking about the reproduction of structures to talking about systems – patterns of interaction: 'the rules and resources drawn upon in the production and reproduction of social action are at the same time the means of system reproduction' (Giddens 1984: 19). He also acknowledges a limitation to the linguistic analogy in that, whereas everybody who speaks the same language shares the same rules, everybody living within the same social system does not share the same rules of social action – societies are not unified in that sense.

Giddens also engages in his clearest technical discussion of the nature of rules. He sets out four examples of a rule, three of which are explicitly formulated and one of which is a mathematical formula of the type which predicts the numbers which will follow in a particular sequence of numbers – for example, if the sequence is 2, 4, 6, 8, the formula will be $x=n+2$, where x is the next number and n the previous number. Of the four examples, Giddens claims that the mathematical formula is the closest to what he means by the rules of social life. The three that are formulated explicitly are already interpreted in some way and enter into the arguments about interpretation that can place any act under or outside the rubric of a rule. Law courts and tax offices are good places to witness the many different ways in which any particular rule can be interpreted, however clearly it is formulated. Mathematical formulae are not open to such debate.

How, then, is a mathematical formula like a rule of social action? For Giddens it is, in the first place, because understanding the formula enables us to understand how to proceed in an established sequence. Similarly, understanding a rule of social life enables us to proceed in an established, routine way. Secondly, understanding a mathematical formula is not a matter of explicit formulation – I can state the formula without knowing what it means, and I can grasp the sequence of numbers without necessarily being able to explicitly formulate the principle. Social rules are implicit, taken-for-granted procedures, the 'know-how' of carrying on in established ways which can be applied in a range of different contexts.

Giddens goes on to suggest a number of dimensions along which the rules of social life can be analysed: intensive/shallow; tacit/discursive; informal/formalised; weakly sanctioned/ strongly sanctioned. These are, I think, self-explanatory. Giddens argues that many apparently trivial rules – I think a good example would be the conversational rule about organising turn-taking so that only one person speaks at the same time – are in fact intensive and more important than abstract, formulated rules such as the law against murder, in the sense that they contribute much more to the maintenance of the fabric of everyday life.

Resources

Giddens has comparatively little to say about resources on an abstract level, as elements in a structure, and what he does have to say takes us in the direction of systems analysis. In *Central Problems in Social Theory* (1979a), he says that he includes resources to emphasise the centrality of power to structuration theory, which he opposes to the way power is dealt with in other approaches. In *The Constitution of Society* (1984), he says that we cannot conceive of rules without resources since the latter actually provide the means by which transformative rules are incorporated into social practices. I take this as meaning that the rules must have some sort of 'material' to which they apply. At the same time, it is difficult to see how we could conceive of resources not defined as such through rules. He makes a distinction between what he calls 'allocative' and 'authoritative' resources, often criticising Marxism and evolutionary theories for concentrating too much on the former and neglecting the importance of the latter. Allocative resources comprise the material features of the environment, the means of production and produced goods; authoritative resources comprise the organisation of social time–space, the production and reproduction of the body and the organisation of life-chances. This distinction leads to further distinctions when we come to the analysis of social systems.

Time and space

Comments about time and space have cropped up periodically, and a central aspect of structuration theory is the emphasis that Giddens places on both. They are central at all levels of his theory, and one of the ways in which he defines structures and rules is in terms of what he calls the 'binding' of time and space. This clearly needs further elucidation. Giddens often asserts that sociology, and social theory in particular, has taken very little account of the importance of time and space. He is particularly critical of the distinction between synchrony and diachrony (basically, between static structural 'snapshots' of systems and the analysis of the way systems change over time) which he attributes to both structural-functionalism and structuralism. This, he argues, identifies time and social change; in fact, social reproduction and stability take place over time as well. Any society which exists beyond face-to-face interaction must have means of extending itself over time and space and the inclusion of these dimensions begins, Giddens argues, to break down the boundaries between sociology, history and geography. He identifies three levels of temporal existence relevant to social analysis: the finite temporality of our individual lives; the temporality of face-to-face interactions; and the 'long duree' of institutional time.

When Giddens writes at an abstract level about structures binding time and space, I understand him as not just referring to the cohesion of social systems over time and space, but also to the organisation of our basic stream of experience into something comparatively stable – the movement, in Heidegger's terms, from the ontological to the ontic, the way in which the world becomes

organised around us. It is related to our most fundamental level
of existence.

Structures of signification, domination and legitimation

There are three central structures which emerge from the properties of action itself. First there is the structure of signification,
which is produced by and enables people to communicate with
each other. Structure and action are mediated – brought together
– in the process of social reproduction by 'modalities', in this case
'interpretative schemes'. As far as I understand it, the idea is that
in communicating with, understanding, each other, we draw
upon interpretative schemes which in turn depend upon
structures of signification; whenever we interpret a communication, we not only draw upon these schemes and structures but
also reproduce and perhaps transform them.

The second structure stems from the inherent capacity of
action to transform, from the exercise of power; Giddens calls
this the structure of domination, and the modality he calls
'facility'. By facility he means those resources that we are able to
draw upon to influence the conduct of others to achieve our own
ends. The final structure is that of legitimation, emerging from
the inherently normative aspect of action, and the relevant
modality here is the norms of a society or community.

In *New Rules of Sociological Method* (1976), he states that
structures both of signification and of legitimation can be
analysed as sets or systems of rules, semantic and moral
respectively; whilst structures of domination can be analysed as
systems of resources.

Structural principles, sets and properties

These seem to be be subdivisions within Giddens's general
concept of structure, and again take us towards the analysis of
social systems. *Structural principles* are the most deeply
embodied principles of organisation of a society. It is, I think,
difficult to make easy connections between Giddens's abstract
discussion of the nature of structures and his more substantive
analyses of types of society, so I will simply reproduce an
example, without at this point trying to make the connection.
The central structural principle of capitalist society, he argues, is

the separation and interconnection of the state and economic institutions, in which the immense expansion in economic production consequent upon the 'freeing' of economic activity from state control is matched by an immense expansion of the power of the state over the lives of its citizens.

Structure takes on a more concrete meaning in his elaboration of *structural sets*. The identification of structures 'involves the isolating of distinct "clusterings" of transformation/mediation relations implied in the designation of structural principles' (Giddens 1984: 186). His example of a central structural set of modern capitalism is:

private property : money : capital : labour contract : profit

Clearly a process of transformation is involved here. I can convert my private property into money, which I can then use to invest in capital, which in turn enables me to employ labour and make a profit. There are presumably rules which govern these possibilities of transformation; it is also clear that resources are involved.

If structural principles are at the highest level of abstraction, then *structural properties*, or what Giddens later calls elements of structuration and which I take to be the same thing, are the least abstract and involve us even more directly in the analysis of social systems. Structural properties are '[I]nstitutionalised features of social systems, stretching across time and space' (Giddens 1984: 185) His example of a structural property in capitalism is the division of labour: this brings together the general structural principle, since it is a part of the immense economic expansion that develops with capitalism, and much more specific features of capitalist society, the factory floor itself and its organisation.

The examples I have given here are, I hope, reasonably clear, at least as clear as Giddens's discussions from which they are taken. By this stage in his work, he is calling this type of analysis 'institutional analysis', and the same processes can be seen from the point of view of 'strategic action' in which these structural features - principles, sets and elements - are produced and reproduced. The transformations of the elements in the structural set take place only through people acting in and on the market; there are no dynamics internal to and generated by the structural set itself. We are, therefore, not caught up in the process of capitalist production which forces itself upon us; we are rather constantly producing and reproducing it ourselves.

This discussion has already taken us some way into the analysis of social systems. Before following this through in the next section, I want to turn to the issue of structure and constraint, which figures in many of the debates around structuration theory.

Structure and constraint

Giddens goes to some length to defend himself against the charge that his conception of structure emphasises its enabling aspects over and against its constraining features. The criticisms will be discussed later. For the moment I simply want to look at his account of the constraints on human action. In *The Constitution of Society* (1984), he begins with what he calls the 'causal influences' of the body and the material world, although he points out that these are also enabling features. He argues that material constraints apply to everybody and should not be given any particular causal priority.

Secondly, power constrains, as well as being the means by which we can get things done. Giddens argues that the constraining feature of power is experienced as sanctions, but rarely, if ever, are people compelled into action. Elsewhere (in Held and Thompson 1989) he argues that such compulsion only occurs if we are drugged and moved by force. There is always some degree of freedom in our actions, and he is close here to a radical, existentialist notion of freedom. He develops the idea of a 'dialectic of control' – the space that exists, even when resources are not equally available to all parties in a relationship, for some sort of struggle to take place.

Finally, there is 'structural constraint'. Giddens argues that all structural properties have an objectivity vis-à-vis the individual agent, but how far this constrains varies from situation to situation, and he seems to see constraint here largely in terms of the limiting of options. He ends his discussion with a statement that makes his position very clear:

> I take it as one of the main implications of the foregoing points that there is no such entity as a distinctive type of 'structural explanation' in the social sciences; all explanations

will involve at least implicit reference both to the purposive, reasoning behaviour of agents and to its intersection with constraining and enabling features of the social and material contexts of that behaviour.

(Giddens 1984: 179)

Conclusion

In this section, I have tried to outline in a fairly basic way what Giddens means by structures. It should be remembered that throughout his work, structures can only exist in and through social action and that these together comprise the process of structuration that he takes as the name for his theory. We can analytically study structures by 'bracketing' the social action that produces, reproduces and transforms them. More strictly speaking we can study social institutions in this way as the most deeply embedded structural principles. But this is only one part of what the theory of structuration is concerned with.

Reverting for a moment to the Lego analogy, structures may be seen as particularly complicated pieces with many different sides and angles which we can picture as 'growing out of' the base – action – and providing in turn the core for standard pieces of various shapes, sizes and colours with which we can build many different things. These parts include actors, but also other pieces. My discussion of these – social systems – will be divided into two: concepts relevant to systems as a whole and concepts relevant to face-to-face social interaction in particular, where actors and systems are working together.

INSTITUTIONS AND SOCIAL SYSTEMS

Institutions

I am dealing with institutions and social systems in the same section because it seems to me there is a clear similarity in the way Giddens presents them in his work, and the analysis of institutions leads on to that of systems. Institutions are defined by Giddens not as identical with organisations, as they are often seen in common sense and much sociological thought, but as the practices that are most deeply embedded in time and space – in the sense, say, that marriage is an institution. Systems are patterns of relationships constantly structured and restructured in social practices. When Giddens writes about the two forms of analysis, he calls one the analysis of strategic action and the other institutional analysis – the latter being the one which embraces the study of structures and structural properties. We engage in one by 'bracketing' – basically ignoring – the other. I imagine that he prefers *institutional analysis* to *structural analysis* or *systems analysis* to differentiate himself from structuralists and systems theorists. I. Cohen (1989) suggests we need a further bracketing to be able to look at the time–space patterning of social systems. In fact, in dealing with social systems in the way I have chosen, I am not so much providing that bracketing as absorbing institutional analysis and the study of social systems into one bracket, leaving for later the consideration of social practices and interaction.

Giddens's analysis of institutions is most closely associated with his analysis of structures and as Cohen points out – rather critically, I think – this part of Giddens's work is closer to systematic deductive theorising than any other part (I. Cohen 1989). In fact, structural properties seem to take on the same significance as pattern variables in Parsons' work – abstract categories which provide the basis for classifying different forms of institutions. Each structural property leads us to an institution, and clusterings of institutions lead us to different social systems.

Signification

In *Central Problems in Social Theory* (1979a), Giddens states that when looking at signification as a structural feature of social systems, the relevant rules are *codes*. Codes are the means, the sets of rules, by which messages are generated and communication is achieved. The two have a reciprocal relation to each other. In *The Constitution of Society* (1984) he asserts the priority of the semantic, the meaning, over the semiotic, the generation of signs. He also emphasises the importance of *symbols* as distinct from *signs* because, as I understand it, they carry more, or more powerful, meanings. A structure of signification is the product of several codes, and symbols, symbolic orders, have meaning in a number of structures of signification.

As with a great deal of Giddens's more detailed discussions along these lines, I'm not quite sure how important all these distinctions are. The most important aspect of this particular set of arguments is that the 'institutional order' we are directed to study through structures of signification are 'modes of discourse' and 'symbolic systems'. I suspect these are best understood under more conventional labels: world views, interpretative frameworks, belief systems, etc. Giddens emphasises that these institutions cannot be studied separately from issues of power: domination and legitimation. He argues that domination is the very condition of structures of signification since it is inherent in human action. He thus cannot accept, and can have no equivalent conception of, what Habermas calls 'systematically distorted' communication – discourses in which truth is systematically skewed or hidden by power.

When Giddens discusses ideology in *Central Problems in Social Theory* (1979a), he makes some interesting points. He rejects the idea that ideology is a particular type of symbolic order. This is the view which usually juxtaposes ideology to science, falsehood to truth. Since, for Giddens, discursive knowledge of all sorts is, at least in part, actually *constitutive* of social life, it cannot be systematically mistaken. Instead (this time borrowing positively from Habermas) he prefers to confine the term 'ideology' to the mobilisation of structures of signification to serve the sectional interests of powerful (hegemonic) groups. Investigating 'sectional interests' further, he recognises the usefulness of a conception of interests and wants one which does not depend on the actor consciously recognising his or her wants or interests. He goes so far as to suggest the necessity for a 'philosophical anthropology' to understand the nature of 'objective interests', a suggestion which is at variance with the general tendency of his arguments. A philosophical anthropology is at root a theory of human nature, and in particular of the unchanging aspects of human nature. Thus it is possible to argue that there is a philosophical anthropology in Marxism which states that the nature of human beings is to work collectively on and transform their environment, which in turn requires the transformation of human beings themselves. There is thus a basic human nature which none the less allows us to conceive of different types of human being existing in different types of society. Objective interests in this sense can be based on what is necessary to realise that basic human nature: what is in our interest is what enables us to work collectively to transform our environment in the way we desire. On the basis of this, we can go on to develop a 'critical theory' which enables us to identify and criticise those aspects of our society which prevent the realisation of our nature. We shall see later that if Giddens were to take such a project seriously, he would undermine his insistence on the openness of praxis and history.

Giddens avoids the problem here by saying that there is one sectional interest which we can regard as objective and, I suppose, universal: the interest of dominant groups in maintaining their power. The institutional analysis of ideology seeks to show how discursive and symbolic systems relate lived experience to maintain the dominance of one particular group. The ways in which he suggests this occurs will be familiar to Marxists. Sectional interests are represented as universal interests; contradictions are denied or 'transmuted'; and the present situation is treated as if it were natural – following Lukacs, Giddens calls this *reification*.

Domination

Domination involves asymmetries of the resources employed in power relations and is related to sanctions of coercion and inducement. Allocative resources involve domination over objects; authoritative resources, domination over people. The institutional forms of the former are economic institutions and of the latter, political institutions.

This is an appropriate point at which to elaborate on Giddens's conception of power. As ever, he claims to be overcoming that traditional dualism in sociology which sees power either as a matter of individual will or decision, common in Weberian approaches, or as a property of the social system or structure, as in structural-functionalist and some Marxist approaches. For Giddens it is both of these and more. It is a property of action and of social systems. Earlier, I pointed out that he argues that power is logically implied in the concept of action as the ability to do things. In *Central Problems in Social Theory* (1979a), he develops this notion to distinguish between the general property of action, which he calls its transformative capacity, and power, which is involved in the attempt to get some actors to comply with the wants of others. Power relations involve autonomy and dependence and are always two-way, since we all have the capacity for action. Giddens develops the notion of the 'dialectic of control': there is always the potential or real struggle for autonomy, however unequal the power relationship might be.

Legitimation

Giddens prefers legitimation to value-consensus, since it doesn't entail the supposition that everybody, or most people, actually adhere to a system of norms. The institutional order connected with structures of legitimation are legal institutions. Giddens has comparatively little to say about legitimation as such.

Each of these institutions, which for Giddens are only analytically separable, actually draws on all four structural dimensions – signification, authoritative domination, allocative domination and legitimation – but from his diagram, I take it that one structural property is dominant over others. Giddens's diagrammatic representation of this is as follows:

S-D-L	Symbolic orders/modes of discourse
D (authorisation) - S - L	Political institutions
D (allocation) - S - L	Economic institutions
L - D - S	Legal institutions

where S = signification, D = domination, L = legitimation
(Giddens 1984: 33)

Different social systems are distinguished by different 'institutional clusterings' produced by specific structural principles. The association of institutional clusterings with specific geographical locales is, for Giddens, the way in which we identify a society.

Systems

In *Studies in Social and Political Theory* (1977), Giddens sets out his determination to maintain both concepts of structure and of system in social analysis. It is in the context of a discussion of structural-functionalism and General Systems Theory; as in so many of Giddens's arguments, the two tend to get run together, and I am not quite sure what he is saying about which. However, for present purposes, the following points are important.

First, Giddens points out that in structural-functionalist writings there is a formal distinction between structure and system, but one which frequently becomes blurred, the terms coming to be used interchangeably. The structure is the basic institutional framework of a society, which is seen as functioning in a certain way, and the system is the structure plus the function. Giddens's argument is that this type of model might be appropriate, say, in the study of the human body where we can identify and analyse the skeleton, which has an existence at least in part separate from the functioning of the flesh and blood around it. Where society is concerned, however, there is no such skeleton. The structure exists only in the production and reproduction of the system.

In relation to General Systems Theory, Giddens argues that there are three types of 'systemness' relevant to the social sciences. General Systems Theory, for our present purposes, can be considered as the science of 'wholes' – a system is made up of interdependent parts that are somehow kept in the necessary relationship to each other to enable the system to survive. A system is seen as possessing emergent properties over and above the parts of which it is made. Giddens, of course, rejects this idea but translates ideas from systems theory into his own, explaining system reproduction and change in terms of human action rather than properties of the system itself.

He gives a useful example of the three types of sociological explanation corresponding to levels of system reproduction and change. The first corresponds to what systems theorists see as 'homeostatic causal loops', but which Giddens sees as a combination of unintended consequences of action: the 'vicious circle' which connects poverty, poor educational achievement and unemployment. If we find there is a 'controlling mechanism' in this process – he suggests examinations which determine entry to secondary education – we move on to a different level of systemness, that of 'self-regulation through feedback'. If the state intervenes, then we reach the third level, that of reflexive self-regulation.

A point that Giddens develops consistently in his later work, but which is there from the very beginning, is that social systems are open – or at least their 'closedness' is always problematic. He seems to prefer systems as a more specific term than *society*. When we use *society* in sociology, we tend to import the common-sense connotations of the word involving coherence and separation from other societies. Giddens argues that we should look at societies and the relationships between societies in terms of combinations of systems. The systems themselves will be more or less open and perhaps combined in many different ways. In any case, they are not natural or mechanical systems, but patterns produced and monitored by reflexive human action. Apparent 'homeostatic mechanisms' are explained by Giddens in terms of the unintended consequences of action, and there are times in his writing when the very existence of systemness seems to be seen in terms of unintended consequences – they take their place in the range of factors that produce 'social order'.

System integration and social integration

Both structural-functionalism and General Systems Theory, and perhaps most sociologists, regard systems or social wholes as possessing 'emergent properties'. This means, basically, that when a group of people or a group of institutions come together, new properties emerge simply through the fact of combination, properties that do not belong to any of the parts that go into making up the whole. From this point of view it is possible to talk of the system or 'whole' as something different from the sum of its parts and having an existence over and above them. For structural-functionalists and systems theorists, this leads to giving the system or the whole priority over the parts, which are in turn seen as operating to maintain the system as a whole. The 'problem of order' in its most general sense is thus solved: social order exists because the social whole or the social system possesses a unity and life of its own.

Now it must be clear from practically everything I have said about Giddens that this is not acceptable to him. The integration of social systems is something which is constantly reproduced by the action of agents. How social order happens is then a problem to which he seems to give a number of answers. The existence of structures embedded in social practices, presumably through processes of socialisation, is one answer. Within a social system, we all produce and reproduce the same structures, although as I noted above, Giddens sees that this has its limits, and there must be other factors at work. A second answer comes in the distinction between social and system integration.

Integration is seen primarily in terms of reciprocity, and the basic definition of social integration is the reciprocity between actors; of system integration, reciprocity between groups and collectivities. Giddens also formulates reciprocity in terms of relations of dependence and independence. Social integration is achieved through the reflexive monitoring of action. This seems to mean that in my day-to-day relationships I consciously 'fit in' with other people, negotiating problematic areas and perhaps engaging in conflict where I think necessary. Social order would break down if I made no attempt to fit in at all. Although in *Central Problems in Social Theory* (1979a) Giddens warns us to be wary of the idea that face-to-face interaction represents 'society in miniature', he goes on to say that the 'systemness' of social integration is *'fundamental to the systemness of society as a whole'* (Giddens 1979a:77; emphasis in original). Clearly the achievement of reciprocity in face-to-face interaction is another source of social order.

In *The Constitution of Society* (1984), Giddens defines the crucial difference between social and system integration which really should make us wary of treating the latter as a large version of face-to-face interaction. System integration involves reciprocity across time and space, whereas the defining feature of social integration is that it is face-to-face. The mechanisms by which integration is achieved across time and space clearly involve a difference between social and system integration, and it would be easy (despite Giddens's assertions to the contrary) to see these mechanisms as emergent properties of the system.

I. Cohen (1989) rightly focuses attention on the meaning of integration – it is not the absence of conflict, but the absence of a breakdown in the social order; if a system is integrated, it continues, at least in principle, in much the same way as the established mathematical sequence.

Contradiction and conflict

As I have said already, and will doubtless say again, it is precisely the 'openness' of Giddens's theory, the lack of logical, deductive coherence, that makes it difficult to get hold of. In this account I find myself constantly straining to give it a coherence that is not there. My reason for dealing with contradiction and conflict here stems less from the fact that it follows on logically from what I have just said than that I have mentioned the issue of conflict – that 'integration' does not imply the absence of conflict, neither does it imply the absence of contradiction. Indeed, the notion of contradiction is something that Giddens takes from Marx, and, in *Central Problems in Social Theory* (1979a), he claims to be offering the opposite injunction to that offered by functionalism: Don't look for functions, look for contradictions.

A contradiction is defined as a disjunction of the structural principles of system organisation. In capitalism, Giddens argues, Marx identified the central contradiction in structural principles as that between socialised production and private appropriation: we produce collectively and are mutually interdependent in so doing, yet the results of our production are appropriated by private individuals. From this primary contradiction, Giddens argues, stem secondary contradictions, the major one of which is between the power of the nation–state and the increasingly international nature of capital. Such a central contradiction embodies possibilities of change, not only towards socialism but towards what Giddens calls system degeneration – in this case the development of right-wing totalitarianism. He emphasises that system contradiction actually implies system integration; capitalism might involve a contradiction but it is still a system. The structural principles involved operate in terms of each other but none the less contradict each other. Conflict, of course, involves agents, and although contradiction and conflict tend to coincide, there are various processes which can intervene to make this less likely – depending, for example, on the extent of actors' knowledgeability. Throughout Giddens emphasises that contradictions are produced and reproduced in social practices, and he prefers the adjective *contradictory* to the noun *contradiction*.

In *The Constitution of Society* (1984), and elsewhere, Giddens relates the idea of structural contradiction to that of existential contradiction, and he argues that the three types of society with which he is concerned (tribal societies, class-divided societies and class societies – to be elaborated in the next chapter) can be characterised in terms of existential and structural contradictions. In tribal societies the existential contradiction is central, and in class societies the structural contradiction is central. In class-divided societies, both play an important role. Generally, the existential contradiction is weakened by the appearance of structural contradiction, and this involves the weakening of the links between human life and nature.

Time-space and social systems

I said earlier that for Giddens, system integration depends on the binding of time and space, the reproduction of patterns of interaction across time and space. This means, broadly, that social order depends upon my doing more or less the same things tomorrow - get up, go to work, etc. - as I did today, yesterday and the day before; it also depends on people in Scotland doing much the same sort of thing, and myself carrying on in much the same way when I go to Scotland. What makes this possible is structure in the sense of taken-for-granted knowledge of how to proceed, and when Giddens talks about structures 'binding' time and space, he means that they enable these procedures to continue over shorter or longer periods of time across smaller or larger expanses of space.

In looking at the ingredients of Giddens's omelette, I mentioned briefly time-geography. What modern time-geography enables is the construction of patterns of routine movements through time and space - when I get up and travel to work, I am moving through both dimensions - and social interaction can be seen as the intersection of individuals' time-space charts. As Cohen (1989) points out, Giddens adds to this simple process of model construction a range of other factors that sociologists generally regard as significant in social interaction. However, the construction of such charts does provide a way of describing social systems, although when it is systems we are concerned with, it is less the movements of individuals with which we are concerned than institutionalised patterns of time-space movement.

Of the three sorts of time I mentioned earlier, two - the time of the interactional encounter and the 'long duree' of the system - are what Giddens calls 'reversible time', time which moves in cycles and repeats itself. The time of my daily routine is in this sense 'reversible'. It must be remembered that systems are not identical to societies: there can be 'inter-societal' systems, made up of two or more societies, and one society itself is likely to be made up of a number of systems, and a system can spread across more than one society. The scope of a system has to do with the amount of time–space that it binds, or rather the extent of its ability to bind time and space. This is what I understand Giddens to mean when he writes of 'time–space distantiation'. It is a feature of modern systems, beginning with capitalism, that they possess much greater time–space distantiation than other types of society – the latter are limited by the requirements of face-to-face interaction. As we shall see when I go on to look at Giddens's substantive historical sociology, the increase in time–space distantiation is put down to increased centralisation, the increased ability to store information and increased powers of surveillance, as well as vastly speedier communication systems, involving not just the transporting of individuals but also of messages.

Giddens develops a number of concepts to deal with the social organisation of time and space. The most important are those of locale and regionalisation. Locale refers to the spatial setting of interaction, and locales themselves are regionalised. In *The Constitution of Society* (1984) he offers a fourfold way of classifying regionalisation. 'Form' refers to the type of boundaries that separate regions, whether there are physical or symbolic boundaries. Regions may vary in 'span' – the degree of space over which they expand; and they may vary in duration – the degree of time over which they exist. Finally, they may vary according to 'character', although I am by no means clear about what that means, beyond indicating that different things go on in different areas: in some societies work and domestic life go on in the same area, in others they do not. Locales are organised in a 'serial' fashion: the way in which activities carried out in one locale at one time will have effects on activities carried out in another locale at another time. Modern systems thus display an extensive cycle of patterned interconnections across space and time. I take it that such a cycle is what Giddens means by a 'reproduction circuit', an interlocking of patterns of interaction across time and space which works to reproduce the system.

At this level of analysis, my impression is that the system is seen as a well-oiled organisation in which everybody's activities dovetail into those of everybody else, and 'feed back to their source' to enable smooth and continual working. Giddens makes it clear that such a working is not simply reproductive but is also the means by which change takes place as well. The example I gave in the previous section of a 'structural set' is also a reproductive cycle (see p. 49).

Time–space and inter-societal systems

There is one further set of concepts that ought to be mentioned here, dealing with inter-societal systems and the relationships between different types of society. Again, I will go into this in more detail when I look at Giddens's substantive historical sociology; for the moment it is sufficient to say that he identifies three broad types of society: tribal, class-divided and class societies. Since he has rejected evolutionary theory, he does not see these as necessarily succeeding each other through history, but as co-existing in different ways at the same time. Since as part of his rejection of evolutionary theory he also rejects the centrality of internal mechanisms of change, so external mechanisms, the effects of other different societies, become more important. The relations between different societies, each of which binds time and space in different ways, take place along what he calls 'time–space edges'. They may take a hostile form, involving war, or involve relations of dependence, or perhaps both. In any case, relationships along time–space edges can produce contingent social change, depending as well on a range of other factors, in one or both of the societies concerned.

In *A Contemporary Critique of Historical Materialism* (1981a), Giddens introduces a set of concepts about time, often incorporated from other writers, which are particularly important in his analysis of time:

1 From Levi-Strauss, a distinction between 'cold' and 'hot' societies: cold societies are, in Giddens's terms, tribal societies saturated in the 'reversible' time of tradition, where social life is experienced as a cycle closely linked to the cycles of nature. Hot societies in contrast are societies which change over time and, in the case of modern societies, change very quickly. This becomes involved with what he calls historicity, 'an active and conscious understanding of history as open to human self-transformation' (Giddens 1981a: 167).

2 From Eberhard, 'world time': this is intended to grasp the fact that an apparently similar series of events or processes may have different outcomes and implications in different periods of world history. As I understand it, world time represents a general context which affects the meaning of the events within it: to take a very crude example, the process of industrialisation in Britain in the second half of the eighteenth century has different

consequences to the process of industrialisation in, say, India in the middle of the twentieth century, even though there might be certain formal similarities between the two.

3 His own concept of historical time, by which I take him to mean the common-sense idea of time measured in years and centuries, as when he writes that tribal societies have a much longer existence in historical time than do other types of society.

4 Again his own concept, 'episodic characterisations', which seems to represent a compromise between abandoning any overall, evolutionary view of historical development and putting forward an idea of historical change as entirely contingent. An episode is a sequence of change:

> having a specifiable opening, trend of events and outcomes, which can be compared in some degree in abstraction from definite contexts.
>
> (Giddens 1984: 374)

Associations, organisations and social movements

There is a further set of distinctions that Giddens makes which draws on practically all that has gone so far in this section, and which is clearly part of the understanding of social systems. Unlike the concepts of systems and institutions, these distinctions refer to actually existing collectivities, and they are bound up with the notions of historicity and time–space distantiation. All three are reflexively monitored collectivities, but in associations there is no attempt to control or change the circumstances of reproduction; people do not see themselves as making history. There is a clear link between associations and the importance of tradition. Organisations and social movements, on the other hand, do try to make history, to change the conditions of reproduction. These, Giddens argues, are 'characteristically' found in class-divided societies. The attempt to control conditions of reproduction depends on the ability to collect, collate and store information, and hence on the development of writing. All this is involved in increasing time–space distantiation. Modern organisations and social movements are imbued with historicity.

Returning now to my Lego analogy before moving on, I suggested that the concepts around the analysis of institutions and systems are, as it were, standard pieces which we attach to the base and more complicated parts of the 'structure' to build various different types of model. The next section concerns social practices and interaction; the concepts here can be seen as the 'working parts' in the model, which in different ways bring together actors and systems and structures to produce, eventually, models that look as though they are working.

SOCIAL PRACTICES AND ACTION

In Giddens's terms, in the last two sections I 'bracketed' strategic interaction and looked at structures, institutions and systems; it is now time to bracket these and go back to human action and the nature of the actor. It will be useful, to begin with, to recapitulate: action, it will be remembered, possesses the ability to transform, but when Giddens is talking about social practices, action which draws on the rules and resources of structures, the idea of routinisation becomes important. This is in many ways the basis of the ontological security of the actor. The actor, too, is knowledgeable, in the sense of possessing either a discursive consciousness of what he or she is doing or the practical consciousness of how to proceed in established situations. He or she is engaged in institutions and systems of interaction patterned through time and space. It is worth repeating here as well that Giddens, when he writes about social interaction, draws considerably on the work of Goffman, translating much of the latter into his own terms of binding time and space. Nearly all the concepts dealt with in this section centre on the idea of social integration, the reciprocity between actors – and this provides the link with systems analysis.

Positioning and position–practices

'Positioning' and 'position–practices' are at the centre of what Giddens has to say about interaction, linking everyday practices with social systems. Agents are positioned along time-space paths (see below) and in relation to other agents. A position is specified by an intersection of signification, domination and legitimation, and carries an 'identity', to which a range of normative sanctions is attached in a network of social relations. This idea is very much like that of 'role' in conventional sociology, but Giddens distances himself from the conventional concept because of its implication that the role is 'given'; in structuration theory, nothing is given but is continually produced and reproduced in social practices. Thus he prefers the participle *positioning* to the noun *position*. He also argues that role is only a useful concept when, as in the theatre, it involves a definite setting and clear normative expectations. The notion of, for example, gender role covers phenomena which are too complex and diffuse for the simplicity of the concept.

Actors' positions in their daily time–space paths are also positions in regions, systems and inter-societal systems. Giddens distinguishes between societies where face-to-face interaction and the social system are almost identical as involving a thinly layered positioning, and modern societies where positioning can be very complex. Actors are also positioned along the life cycle or path, and it is the conjunction of both of these with the 'long duree' of institutions that provides a full understanding of social positioning. All interaction is situated – positioned – and the regular or routine features, which I will go on to elaborate, are also institutionalised features of social systems, and are constantly produced and reproduced in interaction.

At the end of his discussion on positioning, Giddens again takes up the question of limitations on the actor's knowledgeability of system reproduction. He identifies four forms: the effects of social location; modes of articulation of knowledge; circumstances affecting the validity of 'belief claims'; and factors associated with the means of dissemination of knowledge. For the moment, these do not need any further elaboration, but it is worth pointing out that Giddens introduces this notion of limits in the context of interaction, different positionings and power relations. Limitations on knowledgeability are not inherent in action or in social life as such.

I will go on now to build up Giddens's model of interaction from its most basic levels.

Presence and co-presence

In *The Constitution of Society* (1984), Giddens draws on Merleau-Ponty's phenomenology of bodily experience. In our immediate experience, we do not think of our bodies as inhabiting particular dimensions of space and time, but rather as at the centre of space and time which are organised around us according to our present projects and situation. We assume in these projects a degree of ontological security, that the world is what it is and is unlikely to change, or to have changed dramatically since we last looked at it. We assume the same about our bodies, which we use pre-reflectively to achieve things. We 'trust' the world around us and our bodies. Our presence in a situation is expressed in important ways through our faces, and in unspoken communication the face is particularly voluble. This links up with Goffman's work on self-presentation. The significance of the face can be gleaned from the meaning of turning one's back on somebody and the word's connotation, in our society at any rate, of 'self-respect' and 'social honour', the things we lose if we lose face.

Giddens follows Goffman in discussing presence and co-presence: being and being with others. Being with others is rooted in being in our bodies, and particularly in what we perceive and communicate through our bodies. Control of the messages which in Goffman's terms we 'give off' through our bodies is important. Full co-presence actually requires face-to-face contact and full openness to the body and facial communications of others, but as Giddens points out, in modern societies, various forms of mediated co-presence are possible, as in conversations over the telephone.

Encounters

Giddens next takes up Goffman's notion of encounters, not least because of the significance of time and space in their analysis. Encounters are clearly limited in both dimensions. They implicate structures and systems and are implicated in them – Giddens again repeats his warning about taking encounters as the basis of systems, despite their importance. For Giddens, Goffman offers a formal analysis of encounters which has a transcultural validity. He draws a range of concepts from the latter's work which he wishes to employ in structuration theory:

(1) co-presence, which I have already discussed;

(2) gatherings: more than two people co-present in a 'strip' of space–time, in which there is a mutual reflexive monitoring of conduct. The physical context is important for all face-to-face

interaction and is incorporated into the interaction. One of the lessons of ethnomethodology, he argues, is that meaning is contextual and cannot be grasped through formal linguistic properties. If I say 'Watch out!', it can be a threat, a warning that the ceiling is about to collapse or a promise to perform well; which it is will depend on everything else that is going on around me. Gatherings may be loose and consist only of glances; and

(3) social occasions, or more formalised gatherings: these tend to be more clearly bounded and often involve the use of specific equipment – knives and forks perhaps. Many gatherings can take place within a social occasion.

Within both gatherings and social occasions, there can be two types of interaction:

(1) unfocused: everything that is communicated through simply being present in a situation with others – the physical properties of the body and positioning are important here. Sitting with my back to most of the restaurant, others will be able to pick up little from me: the heave of my shoulders might be laughter or tears; and

(2) focused: involving the deliberate co-ordination of interaction between two or more people.

I am following Giddens' exposition fairly closely here, and he situates the foregoing in the context of his general theory in the following way:

I have defined social integration as systemness in circumstances of co-presence. Several phenomena suggest themselves as being most immediately relevant to the constitution of social integration thus defined. First, in order to grasp the connection of encounters with social reproduction stretching away over time and space, we must emphasise how encounters are formed and reformed in the duree of daily existence. Second, we should seek to identify the main mechanisms of the duality of structure whereby encounters are organised in and through the intersections of practical and discursive consciousness. This in turn has to be explicated in terms of both the control of the body and of the sustaining of rules and conventions. Third, encounters are sustained above all through *talk*, through everyday conversation. In analysing the communication of meaning in interaction via the use of interpretive schemes, the phenomenon of talk has to be taken very seriously, as constitutively involved in encounters. Finally, the contextual organisation of encounters must be examined, since the mobilisation of time–space is the 'grounding' of all the above elements. I shall undertake this latter task in terms of several basic notions, those of 'presence availability', 'locale' and the relation of 'enclosure/disclosure'.

(Giddens 1984: 72–3)

I shall follow Giddens's own course.

Seriality

We have already come across seriality in the idea of the linking of different activities in different locales in reproduction cycles. Here Giddens is concerned with the linking of activities in the course of day-to-day life. Borrowing again, this time implicitly from Schutz, he is concerned with the way we cut out, from the flow of lived experience, a discrete series of events or interactions or encounters. This happens via changes in locations, which provide the spatial bounds of interactions, and a bracketing off of time spans. There are a multiplicity of 'markers' that enable us to do this. In the case of social occasions, these are often explicit, like the gathering in a particular room and the chairperson's call to attention at the beginning of a meeting; in gatherings, a whole range of skills can be called on to indicate the beginning and end of an encounter, including talk, eye movements, physical movements and so on. Giddens suggests that the markers may be particularly important when the activity concerned diverges from what might be our normal expectations. He gives as an example the undressing and dressing in private that mark the boundaries of a medical examination. Where the markers are less explicit, their marking is the product of a normatively sanctioned mutual collaboration. There are various ways of indicating that I am not watching, perhaps that I haven't even seen the couple kissing and caressing each other on a park bench, and my companion will employ the same means as well. What enforces the collaboration is that if either of us appears to be studying the couple with the interest that we almost certainly possess, we might be thought of as a voyeur.

Giddens emphasises that the basis for this mutual collaboration lies mainly in our practical consciousness, what one might call rules of tact, an agreement to abide by certain procedures which enable interaction to proceed, without loss of face on anybody's part. Such tact, he suggests, is the basis of trust in the world and the maintenance of ontological security. In terms of the interactional appearance of asymmetries of power, he suggests that the ability to flout certain rules of tact marks off those in a powerful position. Thus if I have a student in my office, another student, on discovering this, will wait his or her turn outside in the corridor; a colleague will often enter and enact his or her business (admittedly as quickly as possible) in the student's presence, interrupting the original interaction. If I do not want this to happen, it is incumbent on me, not on the student, to say so.

This example shows that encounters also involve rules of spacing and of turn-taking. Turn-taking is particularly important, since it is linked with reproduction. It is necessitated by such facts of life as that only one person can be in a particular place at a particular time, and that, within slightly less strict limits, only one person can talk at a time and hope to be heard or understood. This, Giddens seems to think, is at the root of seriality in a range of other contexts, which I suppose must go up to and include the structure of organisations and of systems.

A sign of how important Giddens regards these everyday features of self-management to be is that he endorses a view which he attributes to Goffman that madness consists of the inability to maintain tact (which here he identifies with trust and ontological security), particularly in matters of bodily control and dress but also in the opening and closing of encounters.

Giddens also goes on to take up Goffman's idea of framing as providing the means for sustaining ontological security in daily routines, defining a frame as a cluster of rules which constitute and regulate activities in a way that enables us to answer the question: 'What is going on?'

Regionalisation in interaction

The management and organisation of time and space runs throughout Giddens's account of interaction. Space becomes particularly important when he moves on to the last three concepts mentioned in the quotation: locale, presence-availability and enclosure/disclosure.

In *The Constitution of Society* (1984), locales are introduced after a long discussion of time–geography. Giddens criticises Hagerstrand for concentrating too much on time and for using place in an unproblematic way. 'Locales refer to the use of space to provide the *settings* of interaction, the settings of interaction in turn being essential to specifying its *contextuality*' (Giddens 1984: 118). We can describe locales in terms of physical properties, and Giddens argues that they provide much of the 'fixity' of institutions. Again I am unclear quite what he means by this, but I assume it has something to do with the way in which fixed physical settings make routinised action easier, or perhaps even generate it. However, it is not simply a physical location, the physical features are used to constitute meaning in interaction, and the ways in which this occurs links the intimate and personal to the broader aspects of institutionalisation. I assume this is so because of the taken-for-granted rules of procedure which enable the incorporation of the locale into the interaction. A locale can be a room or the territory occupied by a nation-state, and it is their internal regionalisation that is important for interaction. Locales are regionalised in time as well as space: not only do I have a bedroom, I sleep in it at night.

Presence-availability refers to the ability of actors to come together. Traditionally, presence-availability has been limited by the physical properties of the body and means of transportation, but that situation has been transformed by the development of electronic means of communication. Regionalisation affects presence-availability in various ways – an open office implies high presence-availability, the opposite, perhaps, to a lavatory with a lock on it.

Regionalisation can be analysed first in terms of back and front regions. Again drawing on Goffman's work, Giddens argues that people have a 'deep although generalised affective involvement' in the routines of daily life; they are not simply actors. There are complicated relations between self-disclosure and enclosure and between front and back regions, although perhaps it is more possible for people to feel themselves in the back regions, at a distance from official interpretations of rules and norms. This is more so in relation to official occasions.

Front and back regions and self-disclosure are clearly important in what Giddens calls the 'dialectic of control', the power relations which result from the fact that power is inherent in human action and is never exercised absolutely. Back regions provide an escape from the exercise of power (or perhaps an opportunity to plan its exercise), and the importance of centralised surveillance in modern societies means that keeping part of oneself back from public disclosure can become a part of the dialectic. Giddens also suggests that back regions are important for maintaining a sense of ontological security.

Giddens ends this discussion by suggesting a different charting of movement through time and space to that suggested by Hagerstrand. I do not want to go into this in any detail, but basically he argues that the charting should involve the pattern of return that is actually present in everyday life, as opposed to the linear movement charted by Hagerstrand, so if we start and end the day at home, the chart should show this, instead of showing two different 'stations' for home, one at the beginning and one at the end of the day. This captures the routine nature of everyday life that Giddens can see as a sociologist, but which is perhaps not so important for geographers.

The setting out of Giddens's ideas about interaction, and perhaps especially the concluding part about time charts suggests a modification to my analogy with a Lego model. The last components, connecting all the parts of the model, are actually moving parts or – perhaps even better – rotating parts. However, this analogy is perhaps limiting in that it leads to the neglect of central features of the theory of *structuration*, and as a postscript, I want to correct this neglect and re-assert Giddens's primary aims.

POSTSCRIPT: STRUCTURATION AGAIN

When I say that my Lego analogy has its limitations, I do not mean that it is entirely inappropriate. While setting out this account I have become aware that the theory has two 'moments', different from Giddens's two types of analysis, of institutions and strategic action. These two types of analysis are in fact part of one moment: the setting out of sets of concepts which enable sociological analysis, which enable us to grasp and understand our object of study. Here, I think the Lego analogy is appropriate, and the fact that it does not quite embrace all that Giddens is trying to say is, I think, a sign of the difficulty in matching, if not of a contradiction between, the different moments.

Staying with the analogy, the clearest difficulty is with my characterisation of the last set of components as *rotating* parts; it gives the impression of a model which goes on working without changing, a sort of clockwork system which is constantly wound and rewound. There are certainly aspects to Giddens's theory for which this is appropriate, and if we allow for the argument that historical change is contingent, we could accommodate change in the analogy by saying that the model has to be changed depending on what room we decide to keep it in (depending, in other words, on what else is going on in the world and what is happening in relation to other models). But the other moment, the moment when Giddens discusses structuration theory per se, its basic nature, intentions and assumptions, is one in which he gives a freedom to the moving parts, emphasising the creative and transformative aspects of human action. The moving parts are not simply rotating, albeit in different ways, but constantly making and remaking the model. None of the things I have discussed – structures, systems and their elements, institutions, the aspects of interaction – exist in and for themselves but only in and through social action and social practices. All these things are *done,* they *are* not. The difficulty is that they have to be stopped and sorted out in order to make any sense of them at all. The danger is that, in sorting them out, they take on aspects of objects that really exist in the world like other objects. We lose what Cohen sees as the real and central advantage of structuration theory (I. Cohen 1989): the way in which it remains open to the openness of praxis and of historical change.

When I examine Giddens' historical sociology in the next chapter, it will become clear that these concepts are not there to be systematically applied, but are developed to explain certain features of social change and to be used only when appropriate, unlike, say, the systematic theory of Parsons, the whole of which is relevant to any one piece of analysis.

Chapter 4

Giddens's substantive sociology

In this chapter I want to look at five books that make up the core of Giddens's substantive sociology, works in which his main focus is less the construction and elaboration of theory than the understanding of events and situations in the world. They are not so much empirical research (although Giddens has certainly been involved in empirical research projects) as exercises in the interpretation and analysis of others' research and of historical data. They are all theoretical works in the sense that structuration theory is developed, extended and elaborated, but it is fair to say this purpose does not override that of making sense of the world.

The first, *The Class Structure of the Advanced Societies* (1973), appeared comparatively early in his development, and together with *Capitalism and Modern Social Theory* (1971) placed him clearly in the mainstream of British sociology – a mainstream which he would then begin to change from within, particularly from the publication of *New Rules of Sociological Method* (1976). *Class Structure* is still a book worth reading for its theoretical discussions and insights; it is not merely of historical interest in the development of Giddens's thought, though of necessity that will be a central concern in what follows. It is, as Albrow (1990) points out, the place where we come across the first mention of structuration, not as a meta-theoretical concept but as referring to empirical processes involved in the formation and dissolution of social groups. It is not until *New Rules* that the theory is given what might be called an ontological status. Nevertheless it is possible to see in *Class Structure* some of the concerns which, given the intellectual culture in which Giddens was writing, were to push him towards a major theoretical enterprise.

Two subsequent books were published after the major development of structuration theory that appeared in *Central Problems in
Social Theory* (1979a). They are the two volumes so far published
of *A Contemporary Critique of Historical Materialism*, exercises
in historical sociology of a type which has become particularly
popular over the last fifteen years.[1] Giddens stands out from
others in this area in that his theoretical scope is immense. The
most recent book, *The Consequences of Modernity*, is an essay
looking at the nature of the modern world and the future, less
'empirical' than the others but drawing on historical work and his
theoretical framework. In many ways, this analysis of modernity
is the climax of Giddens's historical sociology.

THE CLASS STRUCTURE OF THE ADVANCED SOCIETIES

The problem of class analysis

We find here some central themes of what was to become
structuration theory, primarily the rejection of any unitary,
simple view of social development and any static, reified way of
analysing societies. The 'advanced societies', Europe and America, cannot be taken as a model for all societies – there are many
paths of development, and class is not necessarily a central
feature of a society. The history of all hitherto existing societies is
not a history of class struggle. Classes are not things but
relationships and processes, and the importance of class is an
empirical matter, something we must discover in each case. If it
turns out that class is important in explaining a large area of
social conduct, then we can talk about a class society. Giddens's
aim is to revise the concept of class away from the old static view
of a class as a thing and the unjustified assumption that it is
necessarily the *central* thing.

The concept of class

The first part of the book consists of critiques of theories of class,
the classical works of Marx and Weber and the more modern
work of Dahrendorf, Aron and Ossowski. Giddens defines the
central problem of these thinkers as coping with the movement
between the complexity of social relationships and the comparative simplicity of a society structured into classes. Marxists

produce a grossly oversimplified model of class society, and Weber and the modern theorists produce models in which there are potentially infinite numbers of classes – the concept becomes too general to be useful.

There are two ways of posing this problem and at times Giddens moves between both. When he is discussing Marxist work, he sees the problem as moving from what I would call the 'underlying' class structure – defined in terms of relationships to the means of production – to the existence of classes as identifiable social forces, the problem of moving from the relatively simple to the relatively complex. When he discusses Weber and the modern theorists, who seem to leave us with the possibility of an infinite number of classes, the issue is how to identify classes as 'structured forms', how to move from the relatively complex to the relatively simple. In fact he settles for this second way of posing the problem, trying to offer a solution which enables us to continue using class as a meaningful concept referring to a 'large-scale aggregate of individuals comprised of impersonally defined relationships and nominally "open" in form' (Giddens 1973: 101).

This is where 'structuration' enters. The possessors of varieties of property and market capacities are *structured* into social classes. Giddens distinguishes between 'mediate' and 'proximate' structuration. Mediate structuration involves:

> those factors which intervene between the existence of certain given market capacities and the formation of classes as identifiable social groupings . . . which operate as 'overall' connecting links between the market on the one hand and structured systems of class relationships on the other.
>
> (Giddens 1973: 107)

Mediate structuration is governed by social mobility; the less mobility there is within a society, the more identifiable are social classes. Giddens regards this as particularly important in relation to property ownership, education and manual labour power, and in fact these constitute the major axis of much discussion about class and mobility in British sociology. Whereas Marxists in particular have concentrated on property ownership and the distribution of wealth, non-Marxist sociologists have been concerned with the ways in which the education system could reinforce or change class structures and the effect on the class structure of the growing groups of non-manual workers.

The sources of proximate structuration, the 'localised' factors affecting class formation, had also been the concern of much sociological work over the previous decades. There are three main sources. The first is the division of labour within the productive enterprise, where what Giddens calls 'technique' is important. The division of labour can consolidate or fragment social classes, and the major effect of technique has been to introduce a division between the manual and non-manual working classes. Working with machines, whatever the level of skill, produces a very different environment from that produced by administrative work. Secondly, there are authority relationships, often overlapping with the division of labour, for example, in the way that administrative workers may be engaged in an authority relationship over manual workers. Finally, there are consumption patterns. This clearly owes something to Weber's notion of status groups; Giddens wants to talk about 'distributive groupings' – groups who share consumption patterns, independently of whether they share some evaluation of their prestige over others.

These, then, are the structuring factors that produce social classes as recognisable and significant groups. Together, Giddens argues, they form a three-class system 'generic to capitalist society': upper, middle and lower or working. Each may possess a class-awareness (a common lifestyle), class-consciousness (involving a recognition of contradiction and conflict) and a revolutionary class-consciousness (aiming at social transformation). The operation of the structuring factors and class-awareness are processes, not static features of social life.

Power

In answer to the question of whether there is a 'ruling class', Giddens suggests that there are elites: groups within the upper-class, structured mediately by social mobility into and out of the elite and proximately by the degree of social interconnection between members. This gives him a fourfold classification according to levels of openness and integration respectively.

Power can then be analysed according to consolidation (the degree to which power is constrained from below) and diffuseness (the degree to which it is restricted to certain issues). This enables a fourfold classification of power, which can be combined with the classification of elites. In examining power relationships between the classes, Giddens is concerned to retain a concept of exploitation, but he considers that the Marxist conception, which is entirely economic, involving the production of surplus value, has too many problems to enable us to use it productively. Instead he suggests what one might call a concept of 'social exploitation' in which one class may exclude members of other classes from the possibility of realising life-chances, through denying them the acquisition of certain market capacities. This denial could be seen, for example, to be built into the education and training systems.

Conclusion

The rest of *Class Structure* considers a series of sociological arguments in the light of this reworking of the idea of class, covering the nature of industrialisation, the validity of Marxist predictions about the development of capitalism, the nature of state socialism and the nature of the 'new' working and middle classes. I do not want to go into the details of his arguments here, beyond saying that they seem to me to confirm the common-sense nature and usefulness of the book. He does not get caught up in the often convoluted arguments that Marxists use to defend their rather rigid conceptions, and equally he avoids the fragmented picture that other more recent theorists present in their attempt to argue against Marx.

We can see many of the themes of structuration theory already in this work, including Giddens's tendency towards elaborate classification. Most interesting for me, however, is his choice of the problem of how we comprehend the movement from a multiplicity of groups to classes as structured forms. The Marxist version of the problem is different: how do we move from a concept of class based on the ownership of the means of production to what might be an empirical diversity of groups? For Marxists, we begin with the structured forms, and the problem is often their empirical fragmentation. By choosing the former path, the idea of ontological depth is lost.

Beyond this there is the emphasis on the openness of history and the rejection of attempts to explain social reality through pre-conceived theoretical categories. The complexity of social reality as a process, rather than a state, takes priority, as does the nature of the modern world as opposed to a general theory of all societies.

A CONTEMPORARY CRITIQUE OF HISTORICAL MATERIALISM

Titled *Power, Property and the State*, the first volume of *A Contemporary Critique* appeared in 1981 some eight years after *Class Structure* and represents Giddens's first book-length confrontation with the outside world after the development of structuration theory. The second volume appeared in 1985. Together they cover a huge area, reflecting the principles of structuration theory in content and style. There is a sort of free-floating attention which makes it very difficult to summarise. There is a lot going on in world history and Giddens seems to want to look at most of it, often through the eyes of two or three other theorists who disagree with each other. If there is a central thesis, it is that social development is not evolutionary but the product of many processes; that extension over time and space is especially important, and the most important factors contributing to social change are those that enable a society to extend itself over time and space; and that the modern world is radically different from what has gone before, the result of changes of 'extraordinary magnitude'. I have tried to integrate my account of the two works under some central headings, approximately covering the 'episodes' Giddens deals with and making it clear, when necessary, to which work I am referring: *A Contemporary Critique* refers to volume one, *The Nation State* to volume two.

A non-evolutionary conception of different types of society

In the introduction to *A Contemporary Critique*, Giddens rehearses his arguments against functionalism and evolutionary theory. We cannot, he argues, see a society as in any way a unified whole with emergent properties of its own, or with some 'essential' centre. Nor can it be seen, as Althusser (1969) suggests, as a combination of different levels: the economic, political and ideological. Why these levels rather than others? Societies, Giddens argues, should be analysed in terms of the institutionalised practices based on the properties of human action as such, and much of what follows is an account of historical change in terms of the interrelation of changes in these institutionalised practices. He then offers a definition of a society as a system (a collection of systems) which is associated with a (not necessarily fixed) locale, legitimated prerogatives – particularly over material resources in that locale – an institutional clustering of practices sustained through social and system integration and an overall awareness of belonging to an inclusive community with a certain identity. The institutionalised practices are, as we have seen, signification, domination over authoritative resources, domination over allocative resources, and legitimation.

His basic point is that Marx's work is most useful as a theory of early capitalism but all his most general statements, about class struggle and the materialist conception of history are simply wrong. In non-capitalist societies, authoritative resources are more important than allocative resources, and there is no linear development to capitalism as the high point (so far). We might be able to find social classes in non-capitalist societies, but class struggle and the contradiction between the forces and relations of production are not central, as they are in early capitalist societies. He calls such non-capitalist societies 'class-divided' as opposed to 'class' societies. He produces a range of anthropological evidence against Marx and looks at a number of arguments from *The Grundrisse* (1973) which run counter to the latter's normal evolutionary view.

In place of evolutionary theories, Giddens classifies societies according to the 'stretch' of time and space that they bind:

Band societies
Settled agricultural communities

City-states
Empires   } 'Civilisations' (class-divided)
Feudal societies

Capitalist societies }
Socialist societies } Industrial societies

He suggests that we should study the interconnectedness of different types of society as a source of social change, looking at proximity in time and space – throughout history we find the coexistence of societies living on time–space edges.

The time–space distantiation of band societies (hunters and gatherers) is low, that of modern industrial society very high. In the process of extension, authoritative resources are more important than allocative resources. The existence of, and control over, storage capacity is important here, especially the retention and control of information and knowledge. The appearance of writing is highly significant, enabling the binding of long periods of time and also the differentiation of centre/periphery relations. Even in the case of allocative resources, storage capacity is more important for the production of a surplus than technological change. In the move from band to agricultural societies, the earth itself is the significant store and crops involve the 'burrowing into time' - i.e. planning. Irrigation agriculture makes for a greater co-ordination of time–space relations.

In all societies after the emergence of civilisations, the city has played an important role as a 'power container' and a central store of authoritative resources. David Jary (in Bryant and Jary 1991) sees Giddens as being generally in agreement with Spengler's statement that 'world history is city history'. In societies of high presence-availability, so Giddens's argument goes, social and system (societal) integration are almost identical - basically the society *is* interacting people. Time–space distantiation produces costs in terms of system integration. In city-states, where there is high presence-availability, power is usually based on tradition. In empires, despite the conscious attempts at centralisation, the local village community remained crucially important - system integration was achieved almost in spite of social integration. Of the three means by which it was achieved, the establishment of economic inter-dependence was least important; military power was more significant, as was legitimation in binding together the ruling elites.

Giddens suggests a more complicated three-fold non-evolutionary classification of types of society, according to the relationship between social and system integration and locale, thus drawing in the issues discussed in the two previous paragraphs:

Class-divided societies

Much of what Giddens has to say about class-divided societies is for the purpose of distinguishing them from capitalist societies and discussing the historical 'episode' that saw the appearance of capitalism. In *The Nation State*, he suggests that class-divided societies are essentially segmental in character. The administrative reach of the political centre is low, such that the members of the political apparatus do not 'govern' in the modern sense.

Tribal society	Tradition (communal practices) Kinship Group sanctions	Fusion of social and system integration
Dominant locale organisation	Band groups or villages	
Class-divided society	Tradition (communal practices) Kinship Politics – military power Economic interdependence (low lateral and vertical integration)	Differentiation of social and system integration
Dominant locale organisation	Symbiosis of city and countryside	
Class society	Routinisation Kinship (family) Surveillance Economic interdependence (high lateral and vertical integration)	Differentiation of social and system integration
Dominant locale organisation	The 'created environment'	

Territory tended to have loose frontiers rather than borders – even where they were clearly physically marked. These societies have a weak level of system integration – the larger ones could even be regarded as composed of numerous societies. To different degrees, war and militarism were pervasive; in the larger states potential military power often existed outside the hands of the state.

A crucial difference between class-divided and class societies is the commodification of time. In non-capitalist societies, he argues, the classification of time was not separated from what he calls the 'substance' of social activities, by which he seems to mean events. The commodification of time, he suggests, is rooted in the Christian sense of time involving a teleological, progressive conception. The production of clocks is seen as particularly important. Time comes to have a double existence – I assume he means a use value and an exchange value – and he is interested in the consequences of this for social life. He relates it in particular to the organisation of work and management. The management of free labour has no counterpart in class-divided societies. The importance of separation of home from work is emphasised.

The small proportion of the population living in cities indicates the comparatively low administrative power of the state – it did not control the day-to-day life of its citizens, and was concerned primarily with the control necessary for tax-gathering. State power was no greater in the city-state than it was for the large-scale bureaucratic empire. Giddens emphasises again the importance of the development of writing for the rise of the state and for surveillance. Administrative power approaching that of the modern world can be found in military and religious settings and in relation to slave labour in mines and plantations. However, the focusing on surveillance as governmental power is a distinctively modern phenomenon. In class-divided societies, politics tended to be confined to dealing with differences among the ruling groups. Deviance could only exist and be controlled amongst the personnel of the state itself, but this should not be read as implying that the rest of the population were secure in their communities. In respect to the ruling groups, the rationalisation of religion was important, although it was not necessarily tied to ethical practices; tradition and the demands of daily life cut across its influence. However, the intellectual hegemony of the administrative apparatus was important.

In these societies, Giddens argues, administration still had important patrimonial rather than bureaucratic elements, with no distinction between the vocational and the private, the monarch leading an expanded personal household and participation being a private right. Even centralised bureaucratic empires retained strong patrimonial elements. Landed benefices were important and administrators were tied to the ruling class. There *was* a ruling class, a lack of class conflict, a *severance* of the political from the economic, low alienability of property (i.e. property could not often be sold), no labour market, and the main sanction was control of the means of violence. This is juxtaposed to capitalist societies, where there is a governing class, endemic class conflict, a separation of the political and the economic, alienable property and labour markets, and the main sanction is the economic necessity of employment.

In class-divided societies, class conflict was rare because of the comparative autonomy of agrarian communities. As for the economic and political, there was no clear sphere of the economic – it was not distinct from other forms of conduct and social relations – and the scope of the political was limited. With the rise of capitalism, the economic becomes distinct and the polity broader, and the two are insulated from each other although the connection is actually closer. In the transition, private property becomes capital.

Some of this becomes clearer if we return to Giddens's argument in *A Contemporary Critique* that Marx is wrong about class-divided societies but right about capitalism. The labour contract is, for Giddens, the fundamental feature of capitalism, with no equivalent in class-divided societies. Separation from control of the means of production puts the wage-labourer in a dependent position of need and conflict. This becomes the major feature in the dialectic of control and puts class at the centre of capitalist societies. Considerable significance is thus accorded to the economic, in particular the transformation of nature, and the intrusion of exploitation and class domination to the heart of the labour process. The 'lateral' expansion of capital and transformation into money capital and the 'horizontal' expropriation of labour from control of the means of production are 'two extensions of transformation/mediation relations' (Giddens 1981a: 122) which result in the extraction of surplus value becoming part of the production process. The separation of politics and economics is seen as important, but he argues against the view that the state is only concerned with guaranteeing contractual economic relationships – its activities cover a much wider area – and against the view that the separation of economy and polity rests on the competitiveness of markets; instead, he argues, it is based on the labour contract. The major difference between class-divided and class societies, then, is that in the former the dominated classes do not need the dominant class to carry on the process of production.

Urbanisation in capitalist societies cannot be seen as an expansion of cities in class-divided societies. In the latter, the city is the dominant 'time–space' container and 'the crucible of power'; in capitalist societies, this role is taken over by the nation-state. In non-capitalist societies, the urban–rural distinction is vital, whilst it is not so in capitalist societies; and the factors forming urban life are very different. Capitalist urbanism is based on the commodification of space and this extends to rural areas; there is no vital distinction between them. In the development of capitalist and industrial societies, the development of the state is especially important in Giddens's view, again distancing him from Marx and Marxism.

The absolutist state

The absolutist state is a political order dominated by a sovereign with ultimate political and military control. In the first volume of *A Contemporary Critique*, Giddens mentions the importance of the centralisation of the means of violence in the hands of the absolutist state, and this discussion is extended in the second volume. He argues that he does not want to look at the modern state as developing out of a decaying feudal order – doing this tends to lead to a progressivist conception of history:

> in which the dynamism of the modern West is traced to a sequence linking the Classical world, feudalism and modern societies. I do not wish to deny that there are unique features in the long-term development of Europe to which we have to look to explain the genesis of modernity. But my main concern is to demonstrate that modern states can be contrasted in a generic way to traditional ones. Thus I do not seek to provide an interpretation of how absolutist states developed out of feudalism. . . . My purposes are more typological and comparative. In indicating just how different modern states are from all forms of traditional state I endeavour to highlight some key elements of the discontinuities of modernity referred to earlier.
>
> (Giddens 1985a: 83–4)

Prior to absolutism, he argues, Europe was a diversity of frequently warring states. With absolutism the state system was transformed in a way that is recognisable from the modern world. Europe became a political order with clear linkages to the nation-state system that was to develop. The state began to take on a more 'pyramidal' character, and this internal consolidation served to accentuate its territorial form. The establishing of congresses of states, concerned with settling their relations with each other, was important, and the concept of the balance of power was a radically new idea. This involved the recognition of the legitimacy of other states and none had the right to universalise its own administration. Each had to acknowledge the sovereign sphere of the others. Some states were able to utilise the new doctrine by war and diplomacy to expand; others did not. This he sees as the emergence of a reflexively monitored state system. New borders, as opposed to frontiers, began to emerge: a substantial alteration of internal and external frontiers was demanded by the expansion of effective control, although the development of borders did not culminate until the nineteenth century. The doctrine of natural frontiers began to emerge.

The absolutist state was still a traditional state, but with features not found elsewhere. There were modifications in political theory: the idea of the divine right of kings opened onto a modern idea of government, 'the ruler being a personalised expression of a secularised administrative entity', and it opened the possibility of juxtaposition to an idea of citizenship (Giddens 1985a: 94).

Three main new elements are involved:

(1) the centralisation and expansion of administrative power: this brought monarchy into confrontation with corporatist organisations. Urban corporations tended to co-operate with the absolutist state, a degree of autonomy being granted in return for the consolidation of broader legal frameworks enabling the expansion of industry and commerce;

(2) the development of new mechanisms of law: the appearance of abstract codes of law applying to everybody was closely connected to the notion of sovereignty; there are no exclusions for rank in such codes. The recovery of Roman law was important, particularly in relation to the separation of private property from the public domain. The beginning of incarceration as a form of punishment also took place; and

(3) alterations in modes of fiscal managements: these stemmed from involvement in large-scale wars. This entailed the large-scale collection of taxes, although the centralising and bureaucratising effects of this were comparatively rudimentary.

The absolutist and nascent nation-states were shaped by a myriad of wars growing in size and destructiveness. Three sets of military development were particularly significant: technological changes in armaments, the emergence of greatly accentuated administrative power in the armed forces – 'discipline' in the modern sense – and the development of European naval strength – partly a result of the technological changes:

The European state system was not simply the 'political environment' in which the absolutist state and nation-state developed. It was the condition, and in substantial degree the very source, of that development. It was war, and preparation for war, that provided the most potent energising stimulus for the concentration of administrative resources and fiscal reorganisation that characterised the rise of absolutism. Technological changes affecting warfare were more important than changes in technique of production.

(Giddens 1985a: 112)

The emergence of standing armies is particularly important. In *A Contemporary Critique*, he has already pointed out that the monopolisation of violence in the hands of the state went with the 'extrusion' of violence from the exploitative class relations of the rising capitalism: basically the idea is that the labour contract leaves the labourer economically dependent, so violence is no longer necessary to force obedience. The absence of any serious military threat from the East is also seen as a contributing factor.

The rise of the nation-state, capitalism and industrialism

Modern society is the product of three separate but connected developments: the nation-state, capitalism and industrialism. No one takes priority. In *A Contemporary Critique*, Giddens argues that the growth of nation-states is predominantly an occurrence of the nineteenth and early twentieth centuries (only Britain going before) as a result of 'the dramatic contraction in time-space convergence' – i.e. modern transport systems, particularly railways. A nation-state is not the product of nationalist sentiments but 'the unification of an administrative apparatus over precisely specified territorial bounds' (Giddens 1981a: 190). Nationalism comes later.

In *The Nation State* Giddens takes up the argument between Marxists and industrial society theorists. For the former, industrialism is a result of capitalism, for the latter capitalism is one period in the development of industrial society. Giddens argues that capitalism was a necessary condition for the development of industrialism, but each has its own distinctive features; conceptually and empirically they can exist separately. He approaches the issue through the works of Marx and Weber, but arrives at his own definition of each. A capitalist society has the following characteristics:

(1) capitalism is the primary form of production of goods and services, and the society is heavily influenced by what goes on in the economy;
(2) the existence of a distinct economic sphere entails the insulation of the economic and political;
(3) this separation presumes institutions of private property;
(4) the nature of the state is strongly influenced by its alignments with private property and the insulated economy; and
(5) that we can refer to the same entity as a capitalist state and a capitalist society indicates the importance of boundaries and boundary maintenance.

Industrialism has the following traits:

(1) the use of inanimate sources of material power in production and circulation;
(2) the mechanisation of production and other economic processes;
(3) the prevalence of manufacturing production 'connecting (1) and (2) in a regularised fashion, such that there are routinised processes creating a "flow" of produced goods' (Giddens 1985a: 139); and
(4) in this regularisation, there is a centralised workplace in which production is carried on.

In the pursuit of profit, capitalism possesses a dynamic that pushes towards economic transformation and expansion; industrialism possesses no such dynamic. In the case of the capitalist society, there is a clear articulation between the economic and other institutions; industrialism carries no such implications – it is neutral in respect of wider institutional alignments.

Capitalist society is a society only because it is a nation-state; such states develop in Europe through the conjunction of capitalism, industrialism and certain administrative apparatuses of government, but none can be reduced to the others. Giddens goes on to discuss elective affinities between capitalism and industrialism, involving the expansionary impetus of the former, the commodification of labour and the expansion of administrative power in the workplace.

He identifies two important periods in the development of the nation-state: from the sixteenth to the late eighteenth century, which saw the conjuncture of absolutism and the early diffusion of capitalist enterprise; and the subsequent period, which links the nation-state and industrial capitalism. This involves two periods of commodification: first, land and products, and then labour.

The commodification of land and products is associated in several ways with the consolidation of the absolutist state:

> The emergence of a guaranteed, centralised legal order permitting and protecting an expanding range of contractual rights and obligations is one; another is the development of a monetary system coordinated and sanctioned by state power; yet another is the formation of a centrally organised taxation system.
>
> (Giddens 1985a: 148)

The body of law connected to sovereignty specifies both a political and an economic sphere – the economic is not a residual sphere but derives from sovereignty. The centralisation of law enforcement is also important. This has consequences for general social discipline.

The solidifying and monetarising of taxation undermined the land-owning aristocracy, further eroding their privileges; but it was also an expression of the erosion of their privileges. Similarly, both express and enable commerce. Unlike in the traditional state, taxation changes the day-to-day lives of state members by demanding that they participate in the money economy. State economic direction was also important during this period.

Giddens emphasises again the idea that although class struggle is rife in capitalism, the ruling class does not require direct access to the means of violence to sustain its power. The means of violence are concentrated in the hands of the state, and the development of capitalism in Europe was connected with the penetration of other areas both commercially and militarily.

He then details the factors enabling the consolidation of the nation-state, beginning with the mechanisation of transportation, and particularly the separation of transportation and communication through the development of electronic media. Also important were the expansion of the documentary activities of the state. The initiation of the collection of official statistics is mentioned and the link made with the inclusion of the social sciences in the reflexive monitoring of social reproduction.

In traditional societies, deviance meant little outside of the ruling circles, and patterns of violence were different – policing was impossible and there were always potential sources of military challenge. From the sixteenth century onwards there was a constant threat from landless labourers which encouraged centralised policing, and there was the beginning of the policy of setting people aside from the general population. Deviance involves the idea of reformation and adjustment. The disappearance of violent, spectacular forms of punishment is a part of all this. Another element is the removal of violence from the labour contract and withdrawal of the military from direct participation in the affairs of state.

Giddens re-emphasises the differences of modern urbanism from cities in the traditional state. The city is no longer a distinct entity but is a created environment 'in which the transformation of nature is expressed as commodified time–space; as such it is the milieu of all social action' (Giddens 1985a: 193). This is followed by a list of the main forms of regionalisation:

1 the distribution of nation-states themselves – core and periphery, etc.
2 the distribution of industry and the division of labour in and across states;
3 the different regional concentrations of population; and
4 the existence of many variations between neighbourhoods and locales.

Giddens suggests three reasons for what he calls the irresistibility of the nation-state. The first is the combination of military and industrial power; the second is the expansion of the administrative power of the state; and the third is a series of contingent historical developments.

Modern society

In *A Contemporary Critique*, he argues that the centralisation of the modern state involves the 'production of everyday life' – regularised social practices. He seems to allow the mass society idea that individuals in modern society are vulnerable, alone and anxious, but tries to trace this to rather different roots. The 'ontological security' of tradition is undermined by the commodification of labour, the transformation of the time–space paths of the day, the separation of home and work, worktime and leisure time, and the commodification of urban land, leading to created space – by this he seems to mean that space loses its association with nature.

The routinisation of life is not embedded normatively in tradition – although residual traditions are involved – but much of life loses its moral and rational content. This results in a comparatively fragile ontological security, control by the super-ego and ego being weakened. This leads to Giddens's emphasis on the 'search for meaning' as being fundamental to human life as one of his major differences from Marxism. He follows this with a discussion of the state in capitalist societies.

The state in capitalist societies

The separation of state and society was in fact wider, in terms of penetration of everyday life, in class-divided societies then it is in capitalist societies. The latter are distinguished by distinct forms of insulation separating the political and the economic. The connection between state and everyday life is much closer and can be analysed in terms of surveillance. This involves the accumulation of information and the supervision of activities. The first generates time–space distantiation, the second power. The two are linked because the former can be employed in the latter. Much of his analysis of surveillance and supervision in capitalist societies is inspired by Foucault, and he also takes up and extends the latter's notion of 'sequestration'. Foucault uses it to talk about the sequestration of the mad and deviant, keeping our lives clear of the things that once interrupted them; for Giddens this extends to areas which once made up the very marrow of our experience of temporality in social relations. Sickness and death are also sequestrated (interestingly, he does not mention birth), serving the 'created environment' over what were previously human relations.

Giddens continues:

> From another aspect, sequestration is only a rather pro-nounced version of the time–space *regionalisation* of activities distinctive of life in capitalist societies. The destruction of the 'public space' of urban life of which Sennett writes is obviously part and parcel of the sequestration of intimacy

(and sexuality) from public view in the enclosure of the 'private household'. For the public activities of *presence* in traditional urban life is substituted the 'absent' public of the mass media.

(Giddens 1981a: 174)

In the capitalist state, the power of the dominant class lies in its control over allocative resources, and the state therefore depends upon processes that it does not control; in class-divided societies, it had maintained control over allocative resources through the threat of violence. The separation of state and polity involves a public sphere of universal rights that seems unique to the West, and technological change gives the state a management function that it did not possess in class-divided societies, involving a range of surveillance techniques. Arguing against functionalist Marxist accounts of the state, he states that it is obvious that state officials have an interest in the smooth running of the economy. The state has an important role, as well, in the face of organised labour and as the controller of violence in a nation-state in a system of other nation-states.

In his discussion of class conflict, Giddens employs his idea of the dialectic of control to look at the way in which the existence of class struggle relates the empirical behaviour of the worker to the philosophical theme of human agency. Class struggle is seen as relating to wage and labour discipline, and he points out that Marx had comparatively little to say about day-to-day struggle, since it contains little prospect of overall social change. Yet Giddens suggests that 'close ties' might exist under circumstances he chooses not to specify.

Citizenship

In both volumes, Giddens spends some time discussing the nature of citizenship in modern societies. In *A Contemporary Critique*, he turns to the ideas of T. H. Marshall, arguing against them in emphasising the open-endedness of history. The context of Marshall's argument is the 'industrial society' thesis, involving the idea that class struggle is no longer a threat to the overall order of capitalist society, since that struggle has itself changed capitalism in such a way as to give the working class an interest in the system. This takes the form of different types of 'citizenship' rights which develop successively: legal rights (equality before the law, freedom of contract, etc.), political rights (universal franchise and the right to political organisation) and social rights (the provision of the welfare state). The achievement of these rights leads to the separation of the economy and the polity: industrial conflict does not become political conflict.

Giddens accepts the importance of citizenship rights for the nature of the liberal-democratic state but argues that such rights do not develop in the linear and coherent way that Marshall claims. Legal rights were the product of class conflict not between proletariat and bourgeoisie but between bourgeoisie and the old aristocracy, and there is nothing comparable to legal rights in class-divided societies. The latter two were the product of organised class struggle, but Giddens points out that they are not simply good things; the integrated working class also provided cannon fodder in the First World War. The process has not secured the separation of economy and polity, which is a shifting relationship depending on all sorts of external factors. Elsewhere, in *Profiles and Critiques in Social Theory* (1982a), he argues that the achievement of these rights as a whole is not a once-and-for-all phenomenon: struggle goes on around them, and the process is reversible.

The argument is extended in *The Nation State*. As resources are concentrated in the hands of a sovereign, so is produced a generalised awareness that power depends upon collective capabilities – it is as if everyone is brought into the fold, into the dialectic of control. It is in the context of this dialectic that citizenship rights develop. The expansion of surveillance entails reciprocal relations between governors and governed, and the greater the reciprocity the greater the possibilities offered to subordinate groups in the dialectic of control. Giddens reinterprets Marshall's categories of citizenship rights in terms of areas of contestation around surveillance:

Civil rights: Surveillance as policing
Political rights: Surveillance as reflexive monitoring of state administrative power
Economic rights: Surveillance as management of production.

These are all bound up with class relationships, and this is the medium through which the rights have been extended and can be contracted.

Nationalism and ideology

Giddens then goes on to discuss ideology and nationalism. Again it is the expansion of state sovereignty which is seen as creating the situation where those within its scope become aware of their membership in the same community. The extension of printing is seen as particularly important. Governing classes have the advantage in the ability to formulate ideas discursively, but also important is the ability to define what is to count as political, the definition of what is in the general interest and the articulation of historicity in relation to social change. *Historicity* is defined as 'the controlled use of reflection upon history as a means of changing history' (Giddens 1985a: 212).

A theory of nationalism should account for its political character, its ideological characteristics, its psychological dynamics and its symbolic content. Beginning with the last, nationalism contains the idea of a homeland as a separate entity with an origin and cultural autonomy. These ideas enter into relation with those of sovereignty and citizenship in various ways. If citizenship rights are poorly developed and the state is embattled, nationalist sentiments might take an exclusive turn; in the opposite situation they might take a more polyarchic form. Nationalism is double-edged.

The extension of administrative unity presumes elements of cultural homogeneity; the conditions involved in the reflexive monitoring of the state are those that help generate nationalism. Dominant classes have less difficulty in presenting their ideas as in the national interest than do the subordinate classes.

In *A Contemporary Critique* Giddens elaborates on the psychological dimensions of nationalism, distinguishing these from the institutional phenomenon of 'interests of state' – by which I assume he means the 'material' interests of the nation-state. He argues that the expansion of capitalism involves the retreat of the area of meaningful existence to the private on the one hand and mass ritual on the other. This involves a more fragile form of ontological security, away from the guarantees of tradition:

> Breaches of ontological security threaten the stability of the ego through the upsurge of repressed anxieties founded upon primitive object-cathexes. In modes of social life suffused with 'primordial sentiments', while there may be no lack of conflicts,

disputes and tensions, the sustaining framework of ontological security is well bolstered. But in conditions of day-to-day life in which routinisation has largely replaced tradition, and where 'meaning' has retreated to the margins of the private and the public, feelings of communality of language, 'belongingness' in a national community, etc., tend to form one strand contributing to the maintenance of ontological security. . . .

In circumstances where radical social disruption, mobilisation for war, etc. . . . the relatively fragile fabric of ontological security may become broken. In such conditions regressive forms of object-identification tend to come to the fore.

(Giddens 1981a: 194)

This identification is with a leader and symbolic figures.

The nation-state and war

Nationalism, the nation-state and war are clearly interconnected, and Giddens argues that the industrialisation of war has created a military system which cuts across other categorisations of nation-states – for example, into first-, second- and third-world states.

During the nineteenth century there was comparative peace in Europe, differences being sorted out through congresses; however, military capability and innovation was growing, its effects being felt in colonial wars. The impact of industrial techniques on warfare was at first through the development of communications, in particular the railways. In the nineteenth and early twentieth centuries, the West was militarily dominant; the military had become professionalised. The two world wars were of immense importance as consolidators and generators of social change, in particular the merging of organised science and technology. There is an intimate link between the nation-state and war:

The nation-state is the prime vehicle of political organisation in the contemporary world, recognised as holding legitimate monopoly of the means of violence by its own subject population and by other nation-states. As possessor of the means of waging industrialised war, in the global context of the continuing application of science to the advancement of military technology, the state participates in and furthers a generalised process of militarisation within the world system as a whole.

Whether this can at some future point be contained is, of course, still completely undetermined.

(Giddens 1985a: 254)

The global system

In *A Contemporary Critique*, Giddens argues that the modern world has reversed the traditional order in which the economic was bounded or limited by the military, and this produces a distinctly new form of inter-societal system. He is suspicious of theories of a world system dominated by capitalism, but in *The Nation State* he has much to say about the global system. He criticises the view that the growth of inter-governmental agencies implies a diminishing of the importance of the nation-state, arguing that the world system is not made up of 'pre-existing' actors who then come together, but rather the very existence of nation-states depends upon the reflexive monitoring of the relations between them – that international cooperation and agencies are a condition of existence of nation-states and of the modern extension of the nation-state system.

He proposes two classifications of types of nation-state. The first organises them according to the following dimensions: (1) focal/hegemonic; (2) adjacent/subsidiary; (3) central/aligned; (4) central/non-aligned; (5) peripheral/aligned; and (6) peripheral/non-aligned. Only the USA and the USSR belonged to the first category at the time Giddens was writing; and perhaps that is now reduced to the USA, since Giddens's definition is that the focal/hegemonic nation-state holds sway over its area. Categories (2), (3) and (5) represent, in decreasing order of importance, subsidiary nation-states within each sphere of influence. 'Central' states, (3) and (4), are second order in terms of military and industrial strength, but still a major force in world politics.

The second classification involves classical, colonised, post-colonial, and modernising states. The latter are divergent forms from the classical nation-state. 'Colonised' states are those set up as a result of emigration from Europe, and would include the USA. Post-colonial and modernising nation-states have less cultural homogeneity than the colonised states. The former are based upon state apparatuses set up by the colonising nation; the latter are those states that have moved, through internal upheaval, from traditional to modern without necessarily being colonised.

The institutional traits of nation-states can be categorised in terms of clusterings of institutions, and allocated places along the following dimensions:

+-   Industrialised economy
+-   Capitalistic production
+-   Political integration
-+   Military rule

(Giddens 1985a: 274)

There is then a characterisation of the world system in terms of Giddens's institutions:

Symbolic orders/modes of discourse	Global information system
Political institutions	Nation-state system
Economic institutions	World capitalist economy
Law/modes of sanction	World military order

Modernity, critical theory and socialism

In both volumes, Giddens is concerned to develop a critical approach to the modern world. In *A Contemporary Critique*, he goes back to the conception of exploitation that he developed in *Class Structure*, one much wider than Marx's economic definition. Rather like power, exploitation is seen as essentially incurable, not to be explained by theories of the distribution of economic wealth. It is essentially a relation between power and freedom, and since power is ever-present we can never be free of exploitation once and for all. Power includes human power over nature, and socialism does not remove it. This leads on to a discussion of the nature of socialism which seems to be based on a real desire (on Giddens's part) to think about the possibilities of transformation. He argues that there should be real attempts to set out what a socialist society should look like, recognising the economic and social achievements of capitalism and liberal democracy and that socialism needs an ethical justification. He hints that perhaps some of this justification might come through looking at what has been lost in personal relationships through the growth of capitalism. Socialism also has its contradictions and must come to terms with violence and other, non-economic, forms of exploitation – such as racism and sexism.

In *The Nation State* Giddens extends the discussion around the four 'institutional clusterings' associated with modernity:

heightened surveillance, capitalistic enterprise, industrial production and the consolidation of centralised control of the means of violence. He argues that considering these takes us beyond thinking simply about the transcendence of capitalism.

There have been many studies of the economic aspects of modern society, while heightened surveillance and violence have received comparatively little attention. These in particular should be the objects of modern critical theory. Totalitarianism is a permanent possibility of the modern state, and he arrives at a definition of the totalitarian state as involving four elements:

1 concentrating surveillance in terms of (a) information coding, documentation of activities of the population and (b) the supervision of activities and intensified policing;
2 'moral totalism': the fate of the political community is seen as embedded in the historicity of the people;
3 terror: the maximising of police power, allied to the disposal of the means of waging industrialised war and sequestration; and
4 the prominence of a leader figure: the appropriation of power by a leader depending not upon a professionalised military role but on the generation of mass support.

Totalitarianism is not an all-or-nothing affair but is linked to less cataclysmic potentialities in modern society. This is followed by a discussion of conflict around the 'institutional clusters' of the labour, democratic, peace and environmental movements which could provide a counterbalance to totalitarian tendencies, and Giddens argues in particular for the need for a normative theory of political violence.

In relation to critical theory, he argues that an analysis of what exists, particularly as it has come to exist in its historical dimension, produces an understanding of possible future transformations. He argues that this is a logical point and it does not lead on to what ought to happen, but then all social analysis is implicitly social critique and has transformative implications for whatever it describes.

THE CONSEQUENCES OF MODERNITY

Giddens's most recent book is an extended essay, again reworking and bringing together many themes from the earlier studies. The basic thesis is that 'modernity' has not yet run its course and that many of the ideas usually associated with the label 'post-modernism' are no more than the working out of the themes of modernity. The aim of the book is to provide a sociological account of modernity that breaks free from the shackles of nineteenth-century sociology. Most discussions of modernism and post-modernism concern themselves with philosophy and culture; Giddens is interested in the *institutional* basis of the modern world.

The uniqueness of modernity

Again, he emphasises the uniqueness of the modern world, and his 'discontinuous' conception of social change. Nevertheless, we can still write coherent history by identifying clear 'episodes' of change. The discontinuities of the modern world are the rapid pace and scope of change and the appearance of completely new institutional forms such as the political system of the nation-state, or the transformation of existing institutions such as the city to the point where they have only a specious identity with what went before. Generally, with the partial exception of Weber, none of the classical sociological thinkers saw the 'dark side' of such changes – ecological destruction, totalitarianism, the possibility of nuclear destruction. They stressed instead the opportunities offered by the growth of productive and organisational capabilities. For Giddens, sociology must grasp both sides of modernity.

Time and space in the modern world

As might be expected, the transition to modernity is understood fundamentally in terms of the transformation of time and space. In pre-modern cultures, time and space were linked together: 'when' was connected with 'where'. The invention of the clock marked the separation of time and space; time became uniform and abstract – an hour here is the same time as an hour there and anywhere else – and this accompanied the growth of a more general uniformity in social life. The 'emptying' of time took 'causal priority' over the emptying of space, which involves the abstraction of space from association with particular places. A square mile here is the same as a square mile there, even though here is rural Suffolk and there the middle of Rio de Janeiro.

Places came to be shaped by social forces existing at a distance from them. Time and space, then, became abstract, standard measures in the modern world.

This leads to what Giddens calls a 'disembedding' of social relations from specific contexts. There are two mechanisms at work in this. The first is the establishment of 'symbolic tokens'. He defines these as 'media of interchange', means of exchange that are, within limits, independent of time and place and people. The clearest example, on which he spends most time, is money. Money possesses what value it has independently of who possesses it where and what is bought and sold. He also suggests 'media of political legitimacy' as another example, reminiscent of Talcott Parsons' notions of the media which enable exchanges across system boundaries. His second mechanism is 'expert systems'. Large parts of our social life are organised by professional experts who possess technical accomplishments that we ourselves do not have. An important part of my life now depends upon the word-processor upon which I am writing, yet I have no idea at all how it works. The word-processor itself is part of my immediate environment but it depends on, is determined by, an expert system the location of which I do not know (and rather hope I will never have to learn about).

Trust

The concept of trust is comparatively new in Giddens's work and essential for understanding modernity. We have to trust in symbolic tokens and expert systems simply to make life bearable. What does that mean? He offers a definition:

> Trust may be defined as confidence in the reliability of a person or system, regarding a given set of outcomes or events, where that confidence expresses a faith in the probity or love of another, or in the correctness of abstract principles (technical knowledge).
>
> (Giddens 1990: 34)

For Giddens, trust is related to absence in time and space; it is necessary when full information is not available. It is bound up with contingency and, in the face of contingency, we attribute reliability or 'probity' to whatever it is we trust in. Trust involves offering a hostage to fortune. It is always in some sense 'blind', stemming from faith but drawing on 'weak inductive knowledge'. In the modern world, trust exists in the knowledge that the world is not simply given or governed by the gods, but a product of human activity, an activity which has considerable transformative powers. It involves the idea of *risk* rather than fortune; risk acknowledges that the future depends upon human action. Risk and trust intertwine to reduce danger, and risk involves collectivities as well as individuals.

Reflexivity

Whilst reflexivity defines all human activity, it takes on a specific meaning in the modern world. The routinisation of life in traditional societies was bound up with tradition, which has its own reflexivity. In the modern world, however, routinisation has no intrinsic connection to the past and social practices are constantly examined in the light of new information. Nothing is fixed simply because it is there, and new information is constantly reconstituting practices. This is especially true of knowledge produced by the social sciences. However, such knowledge does not necessarily increase our control over social life. In those limited situations where social life is, as he puts it, 'separate' from human knowledge, and those where knowledge can be employed to augment rational behaviour, this might be the case. There are three limiting factors to such a use of knowledge: the distribution of power enables knowledge to be placed at the service of sectional interests; changes in knowledge involve, in variable ways, changes in values which affect the way knowledge might or might not be employed; and, finally, there are always unintended consequences of action.

Turning from the institutional basis of modernism to epistemological and cultural dimensions, Giddens asks: have we reached or are we moving towards a post-modernist society? Post-modernism, in epistemological and philosophical terms, is usually juxtaposed to modernism. The latter is seen as the inheritance of the Enlightenment, a society and culture in which scientific knowledge replaces superstition and in which people take charge of themselves and of the world. Post-modernism involves the realisation that knowledge – 'serious', 'provable' knowledge at any rate – is not possible; there are only different ways of talking about the world. Beyond this, it is argued that people are not in charge of anything, rather they are the products of discourse – this is the far extreme of the linguistic turn in modern philosophy – or of social relations. More sophisticated commentators have pointed out that the Enlightenment sows the seeds of its own destruction, and Giddens takes up this theme. It is part of the reflexivity of modernity that the increasing progress of science involves the increasing questioning of science, a relativising of knowledge, and the realisation that there are no guarantees to knowledge. This he argues is not a new social form, a new type of society, but a continuation and logical outcome of modernity. The realisation that there are no absolute foundations to knowledge amounts to 'modernity coming to understand itself' (Giddens 1990: 48). As the remnants of traditional society and thought are cleared, modernity becomes radicalised.

When Giddens sets out the results of this radicalisation of modernity, they turn out to be the very assertions at the basis of structuration theory:

> the *dissolution of evolutionism*, the *disappearance of historical teleology*, the recognition of *thoroughgoing, constitutive reflexivity*, together with the *evaporating of the privileged position of the West*.
>
> (Giddens 1990: 52)

Later in the book he presents in tabular form the positions adopted by post-modernist philosophy and his own positions, which he offers as a conception of 'radicalised modernity' (Giddens 1990: 150). He is concerned with institutional developments which produce a sense of fragmentation and dispersal, whereas post-modernism presents itself in epistemological terms, arguing for the dissolution of epistemology. He sees modernity in terms of contradictory tendencies involving dispersion *and* global integration, whereas post-modernism is concerned only with the former. He sees the self as more than a product of discourse, because of its self-reflexive, self-constituting tendencies, whereas post-modernism talks of the dissolution of the self and the subject. He argues that we have to face universal features of truth claims, and we can still produce systematic knowledge, whereas post-modernism insists on the contextuality of truth. He sees a dialectic of powerlessness and power, loss and appropriation, where post-modernism sees only the former features. He believes in the continued possibility of co-ordinated political engagement, whereas post-modernism does not. Finally, he offers an opposing conception of post-modernity itself: it is the possible transformation beyond the institutions of modernity which, one assumes, reinstates epistemology, knowledge, ethics and the individual.

Re-embedding

Giddens discusses the institutional cluster that characterises modernity and the process of globalisation without, I think, adding significantly to what he says in *The Nation State*. He goes on to develop a set of concepts around what he calls re-embedding, the necessity to pin down disembedded social relations in specific times and places. He distinguishes between commitments that involve face-to-face interaction, and those that don't (which he rather disturbingly calls 'faceless commitments') – the latter involving commitments to symbolic tokens and expert systems which he collectively groups together as 'abstract systems':

> My overall theses will be that all disembedding mechanisms interact with re-embedded contexts of action, which may act either to support or undermine them; and that faceless commitments are similarly linked in an ambiguous way with those demanding facework.
>
> (Giddens 1990: 80)

He turns to Goffman's notion of 'civil inattention' to describe the way we handle much of our contact with others on a day-to-day basis, when most of our interaction is with strangers on a minimal, often simply passing, level. Civil inattention involves intricate ways of recognising others' existence, avoiding contact and displaying the absence of hostile intentions. This is presupposed by trust and the most basic form of facework – although it is difficult to see what he means by most basic, since 'focused interaction' is not built on the basis of civil inattention, but is 'quite different'. Focused interaction with strangers employs a balance of trust, tact and power, and rituals of politeness.

Giddens distinguishes between the trustworthiness of people who are well known to an actor and the trustworthiness of the disembedding mechanisms. We usually have 'access points' to abstract mechanisms through individuals and groups, where faceless and facework commitments meet. Our trust in abstract systems is not simply feeling secure about a certain part of the world, since the expertise possessed by these systems actually creates the risky universe we have to trust. Feeling that our money is in safe hands at the bank is not the same as putting ourselves in the hands of God; the human beings who run the bank actually create the situations of safety and danger that exist for our money. Nobody can be completely isolated from these abstract systems, and access points are particularly important. He describes contacts at these points as involving displays of trustworthiness and integrity with an attitude of calm 'business as usual'. This entails a back stage and a front stage of 'professionalism'. Trust mechanisms also govern the relationships between those within the expert systems. However, the main activity of re-embedding takes place through the facework commitments at access points.

Why do people trust?

The answers are: socialisation, particularly the 'hidden curriculum', the absence of any alternative to trust, and the ability to compromise. Giddens deals at some length with the question of ontological security, drawing this time not only on Erikson but also on Winnicott's (1964) conception of parenting, emphasising the way in which the parent or caretaker produces in the child a sense of reliability and trust in self and the world through producing a sense of reliability in him- or herself. He again links ontological security with routine, and discusses the crucial anxieties that arise when routine is shattered. The maintenance of routine involves constant but often implicit work on the part of actors.

Giddens discusses the opposite of trust in relation to the notion of *basic* trust rather than everyday trust. In the case of the latter, when we are talking about an individual's attitude to an abstract system, another individual or a type of individual, it might be appropriate to talk of mistrust in the sense of a greater or lesser degree of scepticism. In relation to basic trust, however, the opposite is existential angst or dread.

The traditional and modern

According to Giddens, the fundamental difference between pre-modern and modern societies lies in the conditions and patterns of trust and risk, and he clearly believes that in modern society, ontological security is more difficult to achieve.

Traditional societies are societies of comparatively low time-space distantiation; trust and risk are anchored in specific localities. Environments of trust are: (1) Kinship relations which tend towards stabilising relationships in time and space; (2) the local community; (3) religious cosmologies (which can be double-edged); and (4) tradition. Threats to trust, or 'environments of risk', come from natural dangers, the threat of human violence (bandits, warlords, marauding armies, etc); and the possibility of what he calls a 'fall from religious grace' – a religious cosmology can produce a form of damnation as well as salvation.

In *modern societies*, which by contrast are societies of high time–space distantiation, the environments of trust are (1) personal relationships (sexual or otherwise); (2) the abstract systems which stabilise relationships across time and space; and (3) what he calls 'future-oriented counterfactual thinking' as a way of connecting past and present. I take this to mean that the future occupies a much greater place in our lives and perhaps replaces the past of tradition. Environments of risk come from (1) the dangers of the modern world's capacity for reflexivity; (2) the threat of violence from the industrialisation of war; and (3) the threat of personal meaninglessness that also comes from reflexivity.

Abstract systems provide a great deal of security in the modern world, but they also involve a transformation in personal and intimate relationships. Trust in an abstract system is not as rewarding on a personal level as trust in another person. In pre-modern societies, personal relationships could be institution-alised as a form of blood-brotherhood, but were anyway based on honour and sincerity and likely to be called on when kinship alone did not provide the basis for a particular risky enterprise. The opposite of a friend was a stranger or an enemy. In modern societies, the opposite of a friend is an acquaintance, a colleague or 'someone I don't know' (Giddens seems to think that this latter is different from a stranger). Honour is replaced by a loyalty based on personal affection, and sincerity by 'authenticity' – openness and well-meaningness. The impersonality of life in and around abstract systems should not be juxtaposed to the intimacy of modern personal relationships: the two are mutually bound up together, one entailing the other. Friendship can be seen as a re-embedding mechanism.

Personal trust in the modern world thus becomes a matter of work, of mutual 'opening out' and this is clearest of all in the matter of erotic relationships. This in turn is related to the search for identity and fulfilment, the attempt to construct a self. Giddens quotes from Christopher Lasch here, but argues that this search is not only a matter of narcissism, but has its productive, positive side.

Risk in the modern world

Giddens suggests a number of features that give the modern world what Lasch calls its 'menacing appearance'. These are fairly self-evident and I will not go into a detailed discussion of them. The first two refer to the effects of the process of globalisation. Risk is globalised in intensity – nuclear war is a modern risk – and in terms of there being an increasing number of contingent events, beyond our control, which can affect us. The type of risk environment has changed with modernity. The 'created environment' becomes a risk: what happens if a nuclear power station goes wrong? And there are an awful lot of cars around to run me down. There are institutionalised risk environments, like the investment market, which do not exist in traditional societies. There are changes as well in the subjective perception of risk: we are aware of our ignorance and it cannot be converted into certainty by knowledge. Risks are widely known and we are aware the experts have limits.

Giddens believes it is the high-intensity global risks, such as nuclear war, which are the most menacing, the most serious threat to ontological security. Such a risk cannot be tested and it is difficult to think about it for any length of time, yet the repression of anxiety we must undertake in order not to think of it has its psychological costs. There are a variety of possible adaptations to the risks of modernity which are again, I think, self-explanatory: pragmatic acceptance, or 'surviving'; sustained optimism; cynical pessimism; and radical engagement. In a discussion headed 'A phenomenology of modernity', he likens modernity to a juggernaut, certainly beyond control, but one which is full of tensions and contradictions – between displacement and re-embedding, intimacy and impersonality, expertise and re-appropriation, and privatism and engagement.

Conclusion

I shall return to Giddens's discussion of modernity on a number of occasions in the critical section of this book. I think it is significant not least because in this text, he takes up issues that are excluded by his theoretical system, such as a society that is experienced as a juggernaut; this takes us well beyond his early insistence on the knowledgeability, implicit and discursive, of actors. I will argue that his theoretical framework in many ways impoverishes his understanding of modernity and prohibits him from adopting any properly critical attitude towards it. Yet that is clearly what he wants to do in the last chapter, and I will discuss his attempt in the context of his other arguments about critical theory.

GIDDENS'S HISTORICAL SOCIOLOGY

I hope these accounts have shown something about the nature of structuration theory: it is not a systematic theory in the sense that the categories are simply worked out and then applied, nor, on the other hand, is it a theory 'worked up' from a detailed examination of historical episodes, along the lines of, say, Michael Mann or W. G. Runciman. It falls somewhere in between. This has made it difficult to digest and present. The range and openness of the theory has left me trying constantly, and failing regularly, to avoid producing lists of factors that are 'important' or 'significant' – or any other word which implies cause or even essentiality; at times it has felt as if I were producing a politically innocuous history text for schools: lots of things happen in history and here are some of them.

I suspect this difficulty might be a symptom of something more profound in Giddens's work. In the final chapters, I will embark on a critique of structuration theory and, of the books I have considered here, I will draw most on *The Consequences of Modernity*. I will argue that there are aspects to structuration theory that make it more of a symptom of the modern world and inhibit any proper critical understanding of modernity. One aspect of the modern world that I will look at is the way in which it fragments our experience, and Giddens's historical sociology seems to me to reflect that fragmentation rather than find a way out of it. His insistence on the *uniqueness* of modernity and the *discontinuity* of history, at the expense of understanding continuities, undervalues the importance of historical understanding.

NOTE

1 See Anderson (1974a, b), Mann (1986) and Runciman (1983, 1989).

Chapter 5

Empirical sociology and critical theory

In this chapter I want to look at what could be called the two opposite ends of Giddens's theory: its relevance and usefulness for empirical sociological research and its possibilities as a critical social theory. The first might be seen as the bread-and-butter pay-off of structuration theory, and some commentators, in particular Alan Sica (1986), suggest that the theory stands or falls on this issue. The critical status of structuration theory is something that has been Giddens's concern since the beginning, and in fact he argues that it is not the 'opposite' of empirical research at all: an important dimension of the critical impetus of social theory comes through its empirical content.

STRUCTURATION THEORY AND EMPIRICAL RESEARCH

An article by Charles Smith (1983) on the pure-bred beef business in Canada uses some of the more general ideas of structuration theory to look at the economic and interactional aspects of the business. I do not want to go into this in any detail, but it is interesting that in his comments on this, Giddens (1983) says that he would not wish to introduce structuration theory into empirical research in as direct a fashion as does Smith, but would rather lay down some general principles. I think the reasons for this can be seen from Smith's paper itself: it is largely a translation of empirical data, much of it derived from participant observation, into the categories of structuration theory, with one or two of Smith's own categories added where the data does not fit easily. Giddens underlines this attitude (see Bryant and Jary 1991), preferring attempts to use his ideas in a 'sparing and critical' way.

I think I. Cohen (1989) identifies the problem when he talks about the difficulty of developing a research programme in a conventional sense from structuration theory. The theory offers an ontology of social life; it tells us, if you like, what sort of things are out there in the world, not what is happening to or between them; it does not give us anything to test or to find out. Cohen puts this in a slightly different way, pointing out that a body of scientific theory and its associated research programmes develop generalisations at a range of levels, the highest making universal propositions. I think this involves a misunderstanding of natural scientific theory, but that is not relevant here; his point is that the ontology proposed by structuration theory establishes that such generalisations cannot be made in the social sciences, and any generalisation that can be made has a clear historical and geographical specificity. Therefore on principle a research programme cannot be developed. As we have seen, Giddens himself talks about structuration theory playing a 'sensitising' role in relation to social research.

Giddens translates this sensitising role into a series of propositions about empirical sociology that are set out most completely in *The Constitution of Society* (1984). He begins with a summary of the aspects of structuration theory that he considers most relevant to empirical research. These include his emphasis on the knowledgeability of agents and its bounded nature; the importance of day-to-day life in understanding the reproduction of institutions, and of routine activity and ontological security; the importance of the context of action and of position-practices; the variety of possible meanings of constraint; the importance of structural principles in specifying types of society; the centrality of the study of power; and the importance of the fact that the knowledge produced by social scientists can be learnt by the lay actor and incorporated into action. This last leads to his idea of critical theory. It seems to me that this list represents the strongest form of prescription that structuration theory can set down for empirical research, in that it catalogues the elements that make up the social world. Alternative prescriptions, such as that he offers in Clark *et al.* (1990); tend to emphasise some elements as opposed to others, or introduce elements not included in the above list.

Social research, he argues, has a necessary anthropological element to it; the sociologist must understand what is already known by those he or she is studying. Literary style is 'not irrelevant' in this, and the sociologist is a communicator, mediating between different contexts of social life. The depth of this ethnographic moment – he calls it, perhaps unfortunately, 'thickness' – will vary depending upon the subject of research. This involves and leads to his second point, the necessity to be aware of the complex skills that people display in co-ordinating their day-to-day activity; thirdly, the research must be aware of the time–space constitution of social life. He then goes on to examine several pieces of social research. The details need not concern us here. It is sufficient to say that they are not research enterprises undertaken under the auspices of structuration theory, but they can be translated into the concepts of the theory and used to highlight some of the issues with which the theory is concerned. He then goes on to suggest that the researcher can be 'inserted' at any one of four levels:

(1) the hermeneutic elucidation of frames of meaning: research at this level can be both explanatory and descriptive, although it is often mistakenly regarded as simply the latter;
(2) studying the 'context' and 'form' of practical consciousness, and including the unconscious: this level goes beyond what is already known discursively to those being studied;
(3) studying the limits of actors' knowledgeability, the unacknowledged conditions and unintended consequences of their action: this depends upon knowledge of the other three levels, and without such knowledge, Giddens suggests, we are left with structural determinist arguments; and
(4) the specification of institutional orders: identifying the main institutional components of social systems and analysing the conditions of social and system integration.

He argues that the opposition that is often posited between quantitative and qualitative research lies on the boundary between the first two levels and the second two, but his formulation removes the opposition.

Replying to some critical reactions to his statements about empirical research, Giddens (in Held and Thompson 1989) elaborates on the distance between structuration theory and empirical work, again warning against the incorporation of the concepts into research in the hope that it might lead directly to methodological innovations. The research methods adopted should be the ones relevant to the aims of the research, and all methods have their appropriateness. He makes a tentative distinction between *theory* and *theories*, the former working at a more abstract and general level and the latter concerned with explanatory generalisation, by which I take him to mean that they work at a more specific and focused level. He again elaborates on possible research guided by structuration theory, going as far this time as outlining a 'structurationist programme of research'. Such a programme would look at the ordering of institutions across time and space (as opposed to looking at societies); it would look at social systems in terms of 'shifting modes of institutional articulation'; and it would be open to the way in which knowledge influences social reproduction and to its own impact on its object of study. This last takes us again towards critical theory, but again it seems to me that what Giddens is saying is that structuration theory tells us the ingredients of the meal, not how they have been prepared, how they are organised on the plate, or in what order or how we should examine them.

STRUCTURATION THEORY AND CRITICAL THEORY

It is clear that Giddens sees structuration theory as a critical theory, but he means something rather different to the body of work that usually carries that label. The work of the Frankfurt School is critical in the sense that it is based upon some conception of what an ideal or a rational society would look like, and against which currently existing forms of society can be measured and criticised. Such a theory is always 'grounded' in some way, there is always an attempt to justify the critical standards used. The justification might be normative, based on a set of conceptions about what is good, or rational, arguing that the fact that we are human beings who possess rational properties leads to the conclusion that the ideal society is one in which those rational properties can be exercised to their full advantage. When Giddens talks about 'critical theory' it is to reject such a grounding – he desires a critical theory 'without guarantees'.

It is easy to see why such a position follows from structuration theory. If history, social organisation, and praxis itself is open-ended, undetermined in any fundamental way, then to 'root' oneself in a view of human nature or human possibilities which are transcultural and trans-historical would be self-defeating. In *Central Problems in Social Theory* (1979a), Giddens uncharacteristically suggests the need for a philosophical anthropology in which we can base a conception of 'objective' interests which are not necessarily known to the social actor, and he regards such an idea as necessary to what he has to say about ideology and exploitation. However, this is not followed up, and to do so would lead him in directions that I think he would not wish to go: towards system-building, evolutionary theory and perhaps even functionalist explanations. If there is some feature of human life which is transcultural and trans-historical in a positive sense, beyond the simple givens of body and mind and action, - if, for example, we are beings who in some way *need* to develop our powers of thought or freedom - then this becomes a moving force behind historical development and leads us to look at social transformations as more or less progressive and successful attempts to realise our abilities; it also can lead to locating the failure of those attempts in the systems we create and in which we then lose ourselves.

Giddens's elaboration of his own form of critical theory is rooted in his notion of the 'double hermeneutic', by which he means the two-way interaction of agents' knowledge and social scientific knowledge. The concepts and discourse of social science must be rooted in the concepts and discourse of those we study - hence the 'ethnographic' moment necessary in research - but in the analysis of practical consciousness, and of the unacknowledged conditions and unintended consequences of action, it goes beyond that of everyday consciousness. However, the knowledge produced by social science feeds back into actors' consciousness of their situation and is used in their activities and in their everyday lives. In this way the social sciences are intimately and inextricably bound up with their subject matter. This makes sociology and social science inevitably critical. In his *Sociology: A Brief but Critical Introduction* (Giddens 1982g), he adds that sociology is critical because it addresses - it must address - the central problems of our age. Finally, and perhaps bringing him closest to more conventional forms of critical theory, he argues that sociology does not take the society that it analyses as given but asks questions about the types of social change that are feasible, which are desirable and the means we might find to pursue them.

In *The Constitution of Society* (1984), he criticises the 'paralysis of the critical will' involved in interpretative sociology's inability to go beyond actors' meanings, and explores the critical aspects of social science in some greater depth. He argues that there is an important distinction between 'mutual knowledge' and 'common sense'. To gain access to our subjects we have to some degree to share in their mutual knowledge of what they are doing, and this should be treated with respect, allowed its authenticity. On the other hand, common sense, 'propositional beliefs' about day-to-day activities, can be penetrated and criticised by the very use of sociological terminology. Where common-sense beliefs are wrong or inadequate, social science is clearly critical, and this is all the more important when those beliefs are implicated in action. Of course, it is not inevitable that this happens because the social scientific knowledge might turn out to be wrong, or the relevant actors might be prohibited from learning the results of the investigation, or whatever. In this view, the social sciences seem to be seen as critical in much the same way that the natural sciences can be critical: they can tell us what is really the case where, hitherto, we have thought something else was happening.

Replying to critics in the paper I mentioned earlier (1989b), Giddens offers his most elaborate analysis of his idea of critical theory. He distinguishes between four levels of critique. The first, intellectual critique, he argues is relatively unproblematic. This is the normal scrutiny and discussion of research and theory by the scientific community. The second he calls practical critique, and that involves the criticism of common-sense knowledge discussed above. It is part and parcel of the reflexivity of scientific knowledge. He does not accept the view that the social sciences (or any sort of science) provides knowledge which is then utilised by politicians and others to pursue ends that are not, and cannot be, chosen by scientists. This view is usually placed under the heading of 'social engineering', which captures well the idea involved in the application of knowledge. Instead he argues, following Foucault, that social scientific knowledge is actually *constitutive* of the practices of modern society.

The sociologist cannot control what happens to the results of his or her research; they can be employed by different groups in different ways. But the social scientist does have something to say about the *way* his or her findings or ideas become part of social life, in particular the way they are incorporated into the exercise of domination. This is the third level of critique: ideology critique. We have already seen that Giddens sees ideology not in terms of false knowledge, as something which is clearly distinguished from science, but as particular forms of the use of knowledge in domination.

The fourth level is moral critique. He expresses his scepticism about the possibility of grounding such a critique in rationality and about the possibility of consensus around moral values, which he sees as a necessity, or at least a necessary possibility, for the Frankfurt type of critical theory. Instead, he argues, moral argument always involves a combination of the factual and the ethical and cannot be grounded alone in one or the other. The sociologist can of course make moral criticisms, and has to justify them, but cannot do so entirely in terms of the *is*, the factual, or the *ought*, the moral. The justification can never be complete and the argument must continue. Perhaps the most interesting aspect of this discussion is Giddens's designation of the areas which structuration theory identifies as areas where moral critique and political critique are necessary: the issues raised by social movements which cut across class boundaries, such as the women's movement and the ecological movement, and above all, perhaps, the issues raised by the possibility of the democratic control of the means of violence. The 'ought' questions here clearly arise from the 'is'; it is perhaps not completely unfair to characterise this as the opposite approach to the Frankfurt School.

In *The Consequences of Modernity* (1990), he concludes with a discussion of the possible critical attitude we might adopt towards the institutions of modernity. We saw in the previous chapter how he likened modernity to a juggernaut, yet with contradictions and tensions pulling in opposite directions. He asks why modernity has not realised the project of the Enlightenment to produce a world we can control. As answers, he suggests the existence of 'design faults', which can, at least in principle, be corrected, and 'operator failure' and unintended consequences, which cannot be corrected. We cannot, in Giddens's terms, 'seize "history" and bend it to our collective purposes' (Giddens 1990: 153). Yet we should attempt to steer the juggernaut and we can move towards this by envisaging possible alternative futures. The main goal should be the minimising of 'high consequence risks': the growth of totalitarianism, nuclear war, ecological disaster and the failure of economic growth. We need to maintain Marx's position that the desired changes need to be linked to institutionally immanent possibilities; we cannot impose a utopian order from nowhere, but we also need utopian goals.

Thus a critical theory 'without guarantees' must be 'sociologically sensitive', aware of real possibilities; it must construct models of the 'good society'; and it must link an emancipatory politics with a politics of self-actualisation. Giddens discusses again the social movements connected with the institutional cluster of modernity – democratic, ecological, peace and labour movements – and goes on to look at what sort of future alternatives can be suggested and to discuss a 'post-scarcity order', although I am not quite clear what he means by 'post-scarcity'. He points out that scarcity is often socially defined rather than a matter of absolutes, so it seems to mean a change in the social definitions of scarcity and plenty. This order implies, on a global scale, socialised economic organisation, a co-ordinated global political order, the transcendence of war and a system of planetary care. These are the utopian goals, and he concludes the book by describing the differences between this possible post-modern system and the major features of modernity:

> The utopias of utopian realism are antithetical to both the reflexivity and temporality of modernity. Utopian prescriptions or anticipations set a baseline for future states of affairs which blocks off modernity's endlessly open character . . . time and space would no longer be ordered in their interrelations by historicity . . . there would be a renewed fixity to certain aspects of life that would recall some features of tradition. Such a fixity would in turn provide a grounding for the sense of ontological security, reinforced by an awareness of a social universe subject to human control. This would not be a world that 'collapses outward' into decentralised organisations but would no doubt interlace the local and the global in complex fashion. Would such a world involve a radical reorganisation of time and space? It seems likely.
>
> (Giddens 1990: 178)

The last part of this book represents the clearest statement that Giddens offers of a possible society, and in many ways is not that different from what might emerge from critical theory, but there is no attempt at the moral justification that he would presumably also think necessary.

Chapter 6

The trouble with syntheses

In this and the following chapters, I want to go over much of the same material again, from different points of view, and this time from a critical position. For the moment, it might be helpful to reiterate the four lines of criticism that I mentioned in the introduction: the lack of ontological depth in structuration theory, the necessity for theoretical pluralism (which will be the dominant theme in this chapter), the themes of fragmentation and modernity, and the need for a more thoroughgoing critical theory than he manages to develop. Towards the end, Giddens's arguments in *The Consequences of Modernity* (1990) will become very important.

It is perhaps already evident that my reactions to his work are mixed. I sometimes find myself thinking not just that 'the world isn't like that', but also 'sociology *shouldn't* be like that'. The latter reaction is dominant when I read his work as offering an overall synthesis for sociology, an exhaustive description of the social world. He is, as always, moderate in his propositions, acknowledging that because it must reflect social divisions and processes, sociology can never become a discipline with a unitary, accepted body of theory. Nevertheless he argues, for example in *Social Theory and Modern Sociology* (1987a), that certain perspectives will be ruled out and that there will be a consensus at least around the rejection of naturalism and determinist explanations. And there are moments when he dismisses whole schools of thought, structuralism and post-structuralism, as well as positivism, functionalism and evolutionary theory. It is this I find particularly difficult to take, for reasons I shall now try to explain.

IN DEFENCE OF PLURALISM

I have mentioned before that Giddens is often called eclectic. I am, on the whole, in favour of eclecticism. There is no clear single theory for sociology; each existing theory has some part of the truth. To begin with, I want to argue that Giddens is, in principle, not sufficiently eclectic.

My argument has to do with epistemology and the nature of science. I do not want to get involved in setting up criteria of scientificity, although it seems to me that setting up such criteria is part of the sociological enterprise; however, it is only one part which must exist simultaneously with the breaking down of these same criteria, and the use of a range of activities that are, on a common-sense level, non- or even anti-scientific. My warrant here is a book published by Paul Feyerabend in the mid-seventies *Against Method*, in which he proposes an 'anarchist theory of knowledge' with the one rule that 'anything goes'. His argument is built up through an analysis of the history of science, showing how a range of unscientific activities – such as Galileo's rhetorical ability – enter into what is generally considered scientific progress. There are a range of arguments, perhaps not all of them employed by Feyerabend, in support of this approach. There is the history of science itself, on which he is strongest, which shows that science is by no means always scientific. This is backed up by the work of such as Thomas Kuhn (1962) on the nature of scientific revolutions, and by the conventional sociology of science, which is concerned with the social pressures acting on scientific activity.

A theory tells us what to look at: it is like having our attention directed to certain features of the landscape. Other features are seen subliminally or, perhaps, not seen at all. Yet they may have considerable significance. I think this is the case in Giddens's work with his notion of ontological security and routine, to which he gives a fundamental importance. I shall argue later that it draws our attention away from the senses in which routine can destroy our security or offer a false security.

A theory also tells us where to put things. And if they do not fit, then we have to pare them down and alter their shape. We can see Giddens doing this throughout his work. He does it on a theoretical level, taking bits from other people and criticising or ignoring the parts that he does not want – sometimes with bizarre results, such as the incorporation of elements of Lacan into his idea of basic ontological security, an idea which would be an anathema to Lacan. Given that these theories are attempts to grasp reality – and in the nature of things, no ideas which human beings have in and about the world are entirely irrelevant to the world – this is a sort of violence against reality. It removes from sight something which *can* be seen. In the history of science, we can see this sort of process at work in the removal from sight of ideas which are not easily established by conventional methods. The history of the discovery of X-rays, for example, shows how evidence need not be seen or can be discounted when it does not easily fit the prevailing theory.

Feyerabend points out the necessity for science to resort, at times, to the irrational, to 'unreason', whether this be rhetoric or perhaps apparently crazy ideas. In *The Sociological Imagination*, C. Wright Mills suggests, as part of the research, throwing one's notes in the air and seeing if you can make any sense of the way they come down. Unthought-of connections, relationships or ideas can emerge in this way. Giddens throws a fair amount of his notes into the wastepaper basket, and it is difficult to see him being as free with the rest. We have, for example, the option of looking at power in the context of institutional analysis or the analysis of strategic action. There is nothing wrong with this, but might we not learn something from taking 'power' as a starting point, the *essential* feature of human life upon which structure and action depend? I do not think this is right in any absolute sense, but it is conceivable that it might reveal something that is not revealed by Giddens's framework; the historical sociology of W. G. Runciman, for example, shows this well.

Theory can become an end in itself. If I commit myself to a theory, then I have to protect it; my attention is directed away from the world I am trying to understand and towards problems of logic and coherence and towards attacks on my position from other positions. I think there is a process here similar to the taking on of a personal identity. My identity as, say, an academic or a lecturer may serve to hide all sorts of inner confusion, and my fear of this confusion may push me into identifying with this outer role. Similarly, the theory might become the most important part of my life. Everything has to be made to fit it, everything else translated into it, at the expense of paying attention to the world that the theory is supposed to help me understand. There are moments in Giddens's discussions of other writers that suggest this might be happening.

Finally, and perhaps most importantly, I want to look at a quote from Feyerabend that I think sheds light on the critical potential of Giddens's work. Feyerabend is talking about the effects of a scientific education:

> a scientific education . . . cannot be reconciled with a humanitarian attitude; it 'maims by compression like a Chinese lady's foot, every part of human nature which stands out prominently, and tends to make a person markedly different in outline' from the ideals of rationality that happen to be fashionable in science, or in the philosophy of science. The attempt to increase liberty, to lead a full and rewarding life, and the corresponding attempt to discover the secrets of nature and of man entails, therefore, the rejection of all universal standards and of all rigid traditions.
>
> (Feyerabend 1975: 20)

Now Giddens is not presenting a theory as rigid as the scientific theories that Feyerabend is talking about, and there are many ways in which he would agree with Feyerabend's sentiments. Yet the potentiality is there, and it is a relief that sociologists are sufficiently egocentric not to adopt theories proffered by other sociologists. If we adopt structuration theory, there will be things that we are not allowed to think and, depending on our commitment to the framework, things we do not want to think. I am not sure that this is what sociology should be about.

IN DEFENCE OF OLD-FASHIONED OMELETTES

I want to move on to Giddens's rejected ingredients, and to argue that there is in fact something to be gained from maintaining them within the ambit of sociological analysis. None are positions that I would embrace wholesale, but they none the less seem to me to provide a view of the social world that is not provided by structuration theory and which does grasp something real.

Positivism and naturalism

Giddens's rejection of positivism came at a time when it seemed that nearly everybody in sociology was rejecting positivism, whether from a Marxist or a humanist perspective similar to

Giddens's own, and I think there is little point in going back over that debate. To reject the more narrow tenets of positivism, however, and to assert the radical difference between the natural and social sciences, is too easy. Of course they are different, but the natural sciences themselves are different from each other, and the objects they study are different from each other. Yet there are certain points at which their methods and theoretical structure are sufficiently similar for these various activities to be adequately embraced under the label of science. To say that sociology is different from the natural sciences because it has a different object is not sufficient. Similarly, we might not be able to identify universal laws in sociology, but it is at least debatable whether such laws can be found in the natural sciences. The formulation of natural scientific theories involves the specification of the conditions under which laws operate, in the same way that, as Giddens argues, generalisations in sociology are historically limited.

Giddens begins by rejecting positivism, but by the time of *Social Theory and Modern Sociology* (1987a), he rejects naturalism as well, throwing out something in the bathwater that might turn out to be a baby. At times he refers to himself as a realist, but this seems to amount to little more than an assumption that an external 'real' world exists as well as the world that exists in language and in people's heads, whereas what is at stake is the nature of that external world's existence. This becomes clearer if we compare Giddens's position with the 'transcendental realism' of Roy Bhaskar. In a special issue of *The Journal for the Theory of Social Behaviour* (Giddens 1983) devoted to structuration theory, Giddens and Bhaskar are occasionally identified together as leading theorists of the approach. Bhaskar's aim, however, is to maintain that there are important similarities, at certain levels, between the social and the natural sciences. A common feature is that all sciences seek to identify underlying structures and causal mechanisms, and Bhaskar argues that this is what the social sciences are doing when they study what he calls 'societies', what I would prefer to call 'social structures'. The study of transformative action, which he does see in a similar way to Giddens, is, however, something different. As he states in his own contribution to this issue (Bhaskar 1983), Bhaskar would give social structures what he calls a 'firmer ontological grounding', and it is clear from his other work that he believes that it is possible to identify law-like tendencies in social science.

What does this mean for Giddens's argument? First, the rejection of positivism does not entail the rejection of naturalism, which can be maintained in a much more sophisticated way than positivism - and perhaps allows for a positivist 'moment' in explanation, although I do not think this point is essential. More important, if we adhere to Giddens's position, we do not investigate either theoretically or empirically the strong case that Bhaskar sets out to show that in principle we can allow social structures a prior ontological status and that we can identify causal mechanisms. Bhaskar argues that we can do so at the same time as we recognise the existence of social praxis, which we can still conceive in terms similar to Giddens's own. Another way of putting this is that Bhaskar offers us, in a basic form, Giddens's account of praxis, plus an account of other social phenomena - social structures that have an external existence in conjunction with praxis - that do not appear in Giddens's work. Thus, whereas Bhaskar's work does not prohibit the investigation of the nature of praxis proposed by Giddens, Giddens's work does prohibit the investigation of the nature of social structures as proposed by Bhaskar. It is easy to see which approach offers most possibilities.

Functionalism

Giddens's critique of functionalism also came at a time when that approach seemed to be vanishing from sociology. At one time in the 1970s, it might have been possible to ask about Parsons, as Parsons himself asks about Spencer: who now reads him? Giddens's central discussion of functionalism (see Giddens 1977) is subtitled 'Apres la lutte'; yet now, thirteen years later, functionalism is again being defended, in Britain by the Marxist philosopher G. A. Cohen (1978), in America by, amongst others, the sociologist Jeffrey Alexander (1985) and in Germany by Niklas Luhmann (1984). I want to look at two ways of defending functionalism in order to make my case.

A modern Parsonian defence of functionalism

In Clark *et al.* (1990), Turner makes a number of useful points.

He argues, rightly, that Giddens's arguments against functionalism are not original, and that few people, if any, would accept, for example, that explaining a phenomenon in terms of its effects was an adequate explanation, or that we could posit social systems as having needs. He goes on to argue that even for an anti-functionalist such as himself, Parsons' concepts can have an heuristic value as descriptive tools: the notion of functional prerequisites, for example, tells the ethnographer what may be important and what to look for in particular situations. If we treat Giddens's categories in the same way, it is by no means certain which set will offer the best empirical description. In fact, it seems to me that they would offer not mutually exclusive descriptions, but simply different descriptions, each one of which might be useful in a different way. But again we have a situation in which Giddens is trying to exclude one point of view of the outside world; yet with two descriptions, we stand less chance of missing something than with one.

If we look at Alexander's (1985) defence of functionalism, or what he prefers to call neofunctionalism, drawing a parallel between the development of functionalism and Marxism, I think we can see the same thing. He argues that perhaps we should see functionalism not as one systematic and unitary theory but as a tradition of thought, with all that that implies in terms of variations and developments. Functionalist ideas can be employed together with ideas from a range of what were once treated as opposing theories, in particular conflict theory, and they can escape the blanket criticisms to which they were once subjected. He puts forward a series of propositions that characterise this form of functionalism:

(1) Functionalism does not provide an explanatory model, but a descriptive model of the interrelationships between social parts, which can be distinguished from the surrounding environment and are symbiotically connected – although without a priori guidance from a governing part. It suggests multi- rather than mono-causal explanations.
(2) Functionalism is concerned with action as much as structure and with expressive action and the ends of action as much as instrumental action and means; it is also concerned with the degree to which ends regulate and stipulate means.

(3) 'Functionalism is concerned with integration as a possibility and with deviance and processes of social control as facts. Equilibrium is taken as the reference point for functionalist systems analysis, though not for participants in actual social systems as such' (Alexander 1985: 9). He goes on to suggest several different elaborations on equilibrium: homeostatic and self-correcting, moving and partial.
(4) The distinctions between personality, culture and society are important, as are the tensions produced by their interrelationships.
(5) Differentiation is regarded as a major mode of social change.
(6) Functionalism recognises, argues Alexander, 'the independence of conceptualisation and theorising from other levels of sociological analysis' (Alexander 1985: 10).

It could be argued, of course, that Alexander has moderated functionalism to the point where it loses what makes it objectionable, and that it is no longer a distinctive approach. I do not think this is the case, since although he abandons the explanatory pretensions of the approach, ideas that are central to functionalism still remain: the idea of symbiotic interrelationships between parts, the notion of change through differentiation, the possible empirical importance of equilibrium, the distinction between personality, culture and society are all maintained as useful. What they offer is a way of looking at the empirical that *might* show features that are not revealed by structuration theory, or any other theory. Whether this is the case is something which must be discovered empirically, and the answer might vary from situation to situation. To rule these ideas out from the start, largely on the grounds that the explanations are inadequate (as opposed to the descriptions being useful), is interestingly the direct opposite to the open manner of Alexander's theorising.

I want to take as a limited and rather tentative example – tentative because of my ignorance of historical sociology – a self-critical paper by S. N. Eisenstadt in the Alexander (1985) collection mentioned earlier. Eisenstadt refers to his (functionalist) study of the political systems of bureaucratic empires published in 1963 and argues with hindsight that although he recognised that political systems are created or constructed, that they are not simply given, he did not look in any systematic way at the processes of construction and maintenance (which in Giddens's terms would be production and reproduction) nor did he take into account in any serious way the fact that populations are not entirely enclosed within a single system – Giddens's point when he rejects the concept of society as a unit of analysis. He goes on to discuss these issues in relation to 'Axial Age civilisations' of ancient Israel and Greece and elsewhere, which were marked by a tension between the transcendental and mundane orders. I do not think the detail of his discussion is important for the point I want to make, though his theoretical conclusions are.

These posit that the construction of systemic symbolic boundaries is part of the human condition – which I take to mean that we are inevitably, given the sort of animals we are, engaged upon constructing and maintaining systems of interrelationships. The construction is a fragile and constant process, but the resulting systems are not entirely open any more than they are entirely closed. Conflict is inherent in this process.

If we compare this with what Giddens has to say, it seems to me that the two positions are, in principle and fairly easily, reconcilable. We could regard Eisenstadt as adding to Giddens's general conception of human action, bringing in the idea that human action involves a more or less systematic patterning of relationships. Giddens himself clearly accepts this, although he does not deal with it at such an abstract point in his work. They are both saying that systems are created, re-created and changed in the course of human action. Both recognise that systemic mechanisms are involved. There are, as far as I can see, two differences of emphasis. The first is that Giddens constantly emphasises the openness of systems as opposed to their closure, while Eisenstadt is only just introducing the idea of openness. This, it seems to me, is a result of the second difference in emphasis. Because of his functionalist background and framework, Eisenstadt is more likely to have identified the ways in which systems are maintained and their boundaries delineated. The crucial difference is that whereas Eisenstadt can incorporate the sort of position that Giddens is proposing, Giddens rejects the sort of analysis that Eisenstadt was proposing in his earlier work. The functionalist focus on boundary maintenance between systems can (no more than that) direct us towards something that *can* be hidden from structuration theory. For instance, one suspects that Eisenstadt can pick out more clearly the way bureaucratic empires push towards delineating geopolitical boundaries, whereas Giddens, in his emphasis on the uniqueness of modernity and the wrongness of evolutionary theory, emphasises the partial and fragmentary nature of such boundaries. In their different contexts, both are perhaps right.

In another paper in the same collection (Alexander 1985), Smelser shows the usefulness of the idea of structural differentiation in evaluating comparative changes in the education systems in Britain and the United States – a dimension that *could* be hidden from structuration theory. Along the same lines, it seems to me that the distinction between personality, social and cultural systems highlights the experiential conflicts and dilemmas of modernity in a different way to Giddens, that these distinctions enable us to see modernity as more than a relationship between individuals and abstract systems that are in principle the same as each other. It enables a different (or in this case greater) specificity of analysis. But I emphasise that I am not claiming that functionalism is *better* than structuration theory, simply that it can focus attention more clearly on different aspects of the world.

A Marxist defence of functionalism

I want now to turn to a stronger defence of functionalist explanations presented by Erik Olin Wright (in Held and Thompson 1989). This is a defence not of structural functionalism of the Parsonian variety but of functionalist explanation within a Marxist framework, and it is part of my argument about the necessity of perceiving the world as possessing an ontological depth and the importance of granting an ontological firmness, as opposed to a virtual existence, to social structures. Wright is sceptical of functionalist explanations, agreeing with Giddens that in many cases they do not explain anything, and that an explanation is an historical account of how a phenomenon comes into being.

Wright's point, which is taken from the work of G. A. Cohen (1978), is that although functional explanations do not explain in this sense, they do contribute to an explanation of the continued existence of a phenomenon. Wright employs two examples. The first one I am going to discuss here is about the way in which a system can work despite the intentions of the actors involved. This time he takes his example from Jon Elster (1979), perhaps best described as a neo-Marxist, who is himself opposed to functionalist arguments. The important mechanism in this example is the market, and Elster argues that we need a functionalist argument to explain why capitalist firms adopt on average a policy of profit maximisation. The explanation shows which firms survive, not how they come into existence in the first place. The market works as a mechanism which selects out the most efficient and eliminates firms which do not adopt such a strategy. Firms may adopt strategies for all sorts of 'rule of thumb' reasons, but the ones who survive will be those closest to the optimal strategy. This will be the case independently of whether the optimal strategy is known, and the end result will be the survival of firms who adopt such a strategy independently of whether anybody wished such a result. Conscious profit maximisation may improve the efficiency of the system but is not necessary for its working.

Giddens's reply is that it is conceivable that no firm in a market will adopt profit-maximising strategies, and for the market to work in the manner described it is necessary that some firms do so, and hence we arrive back at explanations through reflexive action. It seems to me that he is wrong. Some firms may work to the greater glory of God, some to provide the entrepreneur with enough money to keep his mistress, some to satisfy the obsessiveness of the employer, some for the fun of it – but it is still the case that those whose strategies come closest to profit maximisation will survive and others will not and that the functional control of the market will operate. It seems to me that here we have a system which came into existence historically, and it is quite possible to produce an account of that, but which once established works, through traceable mechanisms, in a way that *can* be independent of the reflexive knowledge of participants.

I now want to develop a more profound and problematic example. Wright draws on the work of G. A. Cohen (1978) in his example. Cohen suggests that we can think of social systems as having not needs but dispositional facts, drawing on a biological analogy. The long neck of the giraffe is a result of random mutations; the fact that long-necked rather than short-necked giraffes exist results from the 'dispositional fact' of the giraffes' environment, which increased chances of survival for those with long necks. Wright uses the example that racism can appear for a range of historically contingent reasons, but its survival can be explained by a dispositional fact of the capitalist system: racism divides the working class, making social control easier. Giddens's argument against this example is that either the continued existence of racism can be explained by individuals' and groups' awareness of its 'functions' – in other words, it would become the result of reflexive, intentional action; or it can be explained in terms of a feedback cycle which is not reflexively monitored. But the explanation is the description of what happens, the way in which the feedback cycle works. It seems to me that we might just be caught in verbal complexities here. If I say that the function of the trade union is to ease the task of capitalist planning and production, and then set out to show how that easing is achieved, how the function is fulfilled, then I am presumably showing how the feedback cycle works, without reflexive monitoring. I want to try to get at the difference between functions and feedback cycles.

Instead of racism, I want to draw on a different example: the 'functions' of trade unions. There is a simple way in which one might argue that trade unions are 'functional' for capitalism, at least during certain periods of its development. They make short- and medium-term planning easier because wage agreements last for a reasonable period; working methods can be controlled and stabilised through agreements; it is easier to agree with workers as a body than with each individual worker; it avoids disruption that might follow arbitrary decisions on the part of the employer, and so on. We can envisage a situation where employers and workers are aware of this and behave accordingly. To talk of 'function' in such a situation is a sloppy way of summarising a reflexive understanding of the situation and the action which follows it. We can imagine another situation in which neither employers nor workers see the benefits, employers seeing trade unions as a threat and workers seeing them as a means to radical political change. We could then envisage a more or less slow establishment of the industrial relations apparatus in which those firms which lead the process fare better, followed perhaps by a general realisation by employers of the advantages, and a decline in the political impetus of the workforce. We could see this in terms of a sort of feedback which is at least initially unmonitored. The firms which arrive at a *modus vivendi* with the workforce benefiting on the market in turn encourages other firms to do the same, with both sides gradually becoming aware of the new reality. I don't think we would need a functional argument here, at least if we take the workings of the market as given.

There is, however, a third way in which we might describe the existence of the trade unions as functional for the capitalist system which takes us beyond either of the first two and beyond the realms of action, reflexively monitored or not. It takes us to the notion of an *underlying* system or structure which produces certain effects that are functional for its continued existence and that are not so much independent of the conceptions of agents but work through those conceptions in a way unknown to the agents. The centre of this argument is Marx's analysis of 'commodity fetishism', a crucial part of which is what he has to say about the labour contract and the mechanisms by which surplus value is extracted – a part of his analysis of capitalism which Giddens accepts.

When Marx deals with the economic dynamics of capitalism, the extraction of surplus value, the accumulation of capital and so on, his 'way in' is through a number of distinctions which are not simply givens to our everyday perception. One of these is a distinction between use value and exchange value, and this is particularly important when applied to labour and the sale of labour on the market. If I sell my labour to an employer in return for a wage, an exchange value, the wage is determined by a number of factors – the minimum I need to keep myself alive to turn up to work in a reasonable state each day, and a number of social norms and expectations about what wages should be. The use value of my labour depends on what my employer does with it, the length of time I am set to work, what I produce and so on. The two are by no means necessarily the same – the difference between them in part accounting for the existence of surplus value and enabling Marx to construct his concept of exploitation. As far as most workers and most employers are concerned, it seems reasonable to assume that this distinction remains unknown; it is not apparent to immediate perception or experience. Our experience of the world is of selling our labour, and we want a 'fair day's work for a fair day's pay' as well as the political reforms that might make this possible. Clearly such a concern does not challenge the capitalist system; in certain, but not all, circumstances, it can contribute towards maintaining it.

There is, I think, a very strong sense in which we can say that the trade unions are functional for capitalism, stronger than saying that they can make day-to-day life easier; they channel conflict in a way that does not threaten the basis of the system, and the better they become at their work, and during the periods when they are successful, the more this is the case. This has presented Marxism with all sorts of difficult political problems from its conception on. This use of the term *function*, referring the working of the system by means of the limited conceptions of agents, conceptions limited by the system, has no place in Giddens's work.

If we now imagine a situation in which some or all the agents are aware of this, it seems to me very easy to conceive of a situation where attempts to employ this reflexive knowledge to change the system fail: there would, presumably, be a great deal of conflict, and we could envisage, on the side of employers or the ruling class, the system imposing itself by means of agents or in the case of the opposition, imposing itself against the wishes of agents. This situation would be more amenable to Giddens's type of analysis, but again something would be lost – the sense that we have in our day-to-day lives, that we can find from looking at historical developments and conflicts and that often limits our political objectives for the future, that we are dealing with something beyond our control, something that is not just bigger than us but working in a systematic way to impose itself upon us. Such a sense may be shared by those agents who are, as it were, working *for* the system: individual employers may find themselves forced into taking actions that they do not want to take simply in order to survive as employers.

One of the reasons I find *The Consequences of Modernity* (1990) so interesting is that Giddens recognises this sense when he talks about our perception of modernity as a juggernaut, something which moves in a systematic way beyond our control. He deals with this in part by arguing that it is not really like that, that there are inroads into it, that in fact it produces the inroads that might be developed to change it. But it seems to me that he cannot grasp it theoretically as a system which does impose itself despite or through our wishes. He cannot grasp it as having an existence and depth different from agency and practical and reflexive consciousness. The only real explanation of this sense of a juggernaut is that it comes because modern systems are big and bind large areas of time and space; but this does not explain their systematism. Nor do the structures (in Giddens's sense) of action: they help us understand the systematism of our actions, not of the system. What I am arguing also throws doubt on the significance of reflexive knowledge.

I shall be going further into these ideas in the next chapters. What I want to do here is suggest again not so much that Giddens's analysis is wrong per se, but that it is only partial. It is wrong insofar as claims to cover everything.

Evolutionary theory

Turning to evolutionary theory, I want to make out a fairly general case, not unconnected with the previous discussion, for retaining a loose evolutionary framework, and to point to evolutionary aspects of Giddens's own work. In responses to Giddens such a framework is often defended, but I have not found anybody defending the hard tenets of evolutionism in its functionalist or Marxist form (see Wright in Held and Thompson 1989; Bottomore and Sayer in Clark *et al.* 1990; and Jary in Bryant and Jary 1991). By evolutionism I mean a view of history which does not give any central place to adaptation (although, as I suggested earlier, we might still be able to work usefully with ideas of differentiation) and which does not insist on one moving force and a necessary development through fixed stages, but allows for regressions and different possible paths, perhaps at different levels. In many ways, even allowing for its immense abstraction and rather complicated variations, I find myself sympathetic to Habermas's idea of an 'evolutionary learning curve' which perhaps different societies deal with in different ways. I will begin with the points made by Wright (Held and Thompson 1989).

Wright makes a useful distinction which we can find in biology between organic growth models and evolutionary development. The former involves the notion of a predetermined process of an organism from conception to death, predetermined because it is genetically patterned; evolutionary theory, on the other hand, does not possess such an inherent teleology - there are no determinate stages and no necessary end state. Mutations are random and their survival depends upon a number of contingent features; one could imagine, I suppose, an environment where it might have been easier for short-necked giraffes to survive.

Wright suggests three criteria which an evolutionary theory has to meet. First, it must involve a typology of societies that can potentially be seen as ordered in a particular direction; secondly, if a society reaches a certain level in this order, it should be less likely to regress than to stay at the same level; and thirdly, there must be some probability of moving forward, not necessarily greater than the probability of moving back.

Wright argues that these conditions do not presuppose some universal teleology, or that all societies must evolve through the same stages. More important, perhaps, there is no reason why the mechanisms of change should be the same at each stage. In the discussion that follows he makes two plausible suggestions about what such a theory might see as important in enabling a society to develop and making it more likely to stay at the new stage rather than regress. One is that when the productive forces of a society have developed, it is unlikely that a society would willingly allow regression to an earlier, less productive stage; and when knowledge has increased, enabling perhaps new forms of control, it is perhaps unlikely that that knowledge would be willingly relinquished. I would add that once such a movement has taken place, it might very well contain its own internal dynamic which increases the likelihood of further development – although I would certainly not underrate the importance of all sorts of contingent and external factors. Neither of these forces need be central driving forces at all stages of human history and, as Wright acknowledges of the former, it is perhaps a comparatively weak force. This, however, does not mean that such a theory does not satisfy the three conditions that he sets out.

It is worth pointing out that Giddens deals with the development of modernity in just such a way: there are internal dynamics which push modern societies forward, not least the process of globalisation, and which are difficult to bring under control or change, not least because of the advantages which modernity brings. Wright in fact argues that Giddens's historical sociology (as well as Marxism) can be seen as an evolutionary typology. There is a clear ordering of societies in terms of time–space distantiation, and his disclaimers about historical teleology and the different mechanisms of change do not make his theory non-evolutionary. An increase in time–space distantiation implies an extension of people's control of authoritative and allocative resources which we should not expect to be easily relinquished.

Giddens's reaction to this argument is to state his disagreement with the third criteria, the implication of some mechanism of change pushing societies along the evolutionary scale – in Wright's words, the implication of 'some process, however weak and sporadic, which imparts a directionality to movements from one level to another' (in Held and Thompson 1989: 93). Giddens takes this as implying some universal impetus such as the desire to increase productive capacity, and he states that this is simply not empirically the case, even, presumably, in its weak and sporadic form. He seems not to take into account Wright's comment about the possibility that different mechanisms might operate at different stages in different societies, which seems to me to be important. In fact there are two replies to Giddens that I would wish to make. The first comes from Bottomore (in Clark *et al.* 1990), who states the minimum claim that societies that better master their material environment do better and are more likely to survive. This seems to me such a minimal but basic truism that it can hardly be denied. Giddens's point regarding the existence of hunter–gatherer societies in situations of comparative plenty which do not seek to increase their productive forces is no reply to this sort of point: they don't need to. My second reply is that once this effort, where necessary, has been made, it can set up a dynamic which can lead to further changes which perhaps needn't be at the economic level at all, or can be at a variety of levels; or it could be that the new situation is maintained or is lost through natural disaster or war or whatever.

What seems to me important about maintaining some sort of evolutionary theory – or, even better, several sorts of evolutionary theory – of the minimal kind suggested by Wright or the much more complex version of Habermas (which suggests that there might be a variety of evolutions going on in different ways at the same time) is that it offers a map – several maps – upon which we can try to base our studies of particular events or, in Giddens's terms, episodes. And of course, Giddens himself draws upon at least one, if not several, evolutionary frameworks in identifying his episodes. Bottomore makes a very telling point. Beginning with Giddens's conception, he argues:

> This conception, although it does have the merit of provid-
> ing a framework for considering, say, the question of a
> transition from capitalism to socialism as the major

transformation of the present age, poses some problems of its own. How, for instance, do we define the 'episodes' themselves? Is some general criterion involved? To take a particular case, should we distinguish as one episode a transition from feudalism to capitalism, or rather the advent of industrial society, as some social scientists would prefer? Furthermore, since the episodes selected are very often the stages differentiated in Marx's theory, how strong is the argument against attempting to link the episodes together in a series, perhaps in a new way?

(in Clark *et al.* 1990: 210)

Wright, and less clearly Bottomore, prefer the Marxist conception of history to Giddens's, but the point I want to make here is close to that of Jary, a sympathetic critic: Giddens is 'overzealous' in dismissing the usefulness of alternative approaches. I think that it is very difficult to avoid evolutionary implications, even if we remain at the level of narrative history, but more so once we adopt an an analytic stance, and such theories are useful maps which come prior to looking at substantive empirical phenomena. We do not have to take them at face value, and the stronger the theory, perhaps the weaker its plausibility in the face of evidence; but also, I would suggest the weaker and more variegated the theory, the more use it is and the stronger its plausibility. An implication of such a theory – which seems unacceptable to Giddens – is that human beings are caught up in imperatives and structures that are not necessarily under their control and that push them in directions that are not necessarily desired.

Giddens's account of modernity, of course, accepts this clearly, but his rejection of evolutionary theory has, I think, an important implication in this connection. He is constantly concerned to emphasise the uniqueness of modernity, how modern society is unlike any society that has gone before. His rejection of evolutionary theory has the effect of emphasising this: it leaves us no possibility of finding or rooting the present in the past. This it seems to me is a feature of the ideology of modernism itself, the rejection of history as a source of understanding and knowledge for the present. Giddens's historical sociology has, then, a peculiar status, for it seems to me to be a denegation: an emphasising of history to deny its importance. I will return to this theme in the final chapter.

IN DEFENCE OF VARIEGATED OMELETTES

I want now to look at at Giddens's ingredients, because I think there is a similar process of rejection of useful elements going on there. He never accepts anything wholesale, which is fair enough, but he cuts off and throws away parts of the ingredients with considerable nutritional value.

Action theories

Much of what I have argued so far has been in support of a view which would reintroduce the dualism which Giddens is attempting to overcome: that there are social structures which exist external to the actor and impose themselves upon us. In the next chapter, I shall argue that, contrary to his assertions, structuration theory is best understood as a very sophisticated form of action theory. His most important ingredients are forms of action theory or philosophy – linguistic philosophy, ethnomethodology, phenomenological sociology, and hermeneutics. Certainly in the early stages of his work, the 'linguistic turn' taken by modern philosophy was very important to him, and I shall later argue that despite his assertions to the contrary many of his ideas are still caught up in the linguistic analogy. However, his incorporation of these philosophies and forms of sociology into his work is, for me, the most attractive thing about it: Winch remained frequently ignored by most theorists, phenomenological and ethnomethodological approaches held sectarian enclaves, and hermeneutics was regarded as yet another peculiarly foreign enterprise. Giddens brought many of the ideas from these approaches into the centre of sociological thought.

With such a wide scope, it is not surprising that a regular point in the critical literature is that Giddens misinterprets this or that thinker. This is not necessarily a bad thing; most of us make a living out of misinterpreting not only people of vastly greater ability than ourselves but each other as well. Here, I am less interested in the detail of interpretation than in the systematic nature of what is left out. I want to argue now that in choosing the ingredients he does, Giddens systematically leaves out of his theoretical omelette dimensions of human action and the actor. This is clearest in his choice of those theories which centre on language as opposed to other dimensions of action. A central feature of the linguistic turn in philosophy is to direct attention away from action directed towards external knowable objects, including other people; it has focused instead on the 'internal' grounds of action, often, as with ethnomethodology, deliberately bracketing off any knowledge of external reality. Giddens does not adopt such an attitude, but he takes into his theory ideas that are crucial to it. Thus when he does come out of theory and approach the political problems of modernity, it is with tools that are restricted, by their origins, from dealing adequately with such problems. I will elaborate on this later when I compare Giddens's conception of the place of the external, material world with that of Sartre.

There is another dimension of action that Giddens at least under-emphasises. The form of action theory noticeable for its absence, a conscious absence since Giddens on occasion conveys that he is not very impressed with it, is symbolic interactionism. He draws a lot from the work of Goffman, who is usually situated in this school, but in his treatment of Goffman as a general theorist, he loses the insight that interactionism offers into the internal dynamics of the individual, in Mead's terms the conversation between the 'I' and the 'me'. This gives the individual a depth beyond the practical and discursive consciousness with which Giddens is primarily concerned. Psychoanalysis offers an even broader conception of depth and internal dynamics, and I shall be arguing at some length later that Giddens sheds these dimensions in his incorporation of psychoanalytic ideas. Even though Giddens is perhaps best seen as an action theorist, the relation between action and object and the nature of the acting subject are not dealt with in their complexity. Despite himself, he becomes a victim of the 'linguistic turn'.

Structuralism and post-structuralism

Susan Hekman (in Clark *et al.* 1990) argues that it is in fact post-structuralism which has successfully transcended the dualism between subject and object which Giddens claims to be transcending himself. I think this is basically correct, in that if we see it as a task to transcend dualisms, rather than simply live with them and use them to add to our understanding of the world, then post-structuralism does it better than Giddens through making discourse the central feature of analysis. Discourse defines and produces subjects and defines and produces the objects in their world; knowledge is produced in and through discourse, and knowledge produces relationships of power between subjects. In Giddens's schema, social practices take on the role of discourse and the dualism reappears in the bracketing of structures in strategic analysis and agency in institutional analysis. My own argument throughout this section will be that the transcendence of these dualisms is always a form of wishful thinking, and it seems to me that Giddens is right not to go all the way with post-structuralism, that he does fail to transcend the dualism between subject and object in his own theory. The problem is that he wants to transcend it.

Thus, while it seems to me that some of Giddens's critical points about structuralism and post-structuralism are well taken, I think he loses something as well, particularly when it comes to his understanding of modernity and the experience of modernity. His pronouncement that these theories are dead (in *Social Theory and Modern Sociology*, 1987a) is clearly premature. Fred R. Dallmayr (in *Profiles and Critiques*) takes up his interpretation of Derrida in a particularly instructive way:

> [H]is (Giddens's) theory of structuration is indebted at least in part to Jacques Derrida's notion of the 'structuring of structure'; his portrayal of structure as a 'virtual existence', a 'virtual order' or an 'absent set of differences' is likewise reminiscent of Derrida's construal of 'difference'. As employed by Derrida, however, the latter concept involves not only a factual differentiation of elements but also a more basic ontological (or ontic-ontological) difference; as a corollary, structuration in its radical sense injects into social analysis a profoundly non-positive, or, if one prefers, 'transcendental' dimension. Against this background, Giddens's treatment appears at times half-hearted. In some passages, the notion of a 'virtual order' seems to imply no more than the contingent and essentially remediable constellation of 'present' and 'absent' factors – or at least a constellation in which absent factors can always be 'instantiated' or applied. Seen in this

light, 'structure' tends to merge imperceptibly with 'system':
the virtual order of structural properties shades over into
Merton's distinction between 'manifest' and 'latent' functions.
(Dallmayr 1982: 21–2)

What Dallmayr is saying is that Derrida is on about something
very different to Giddens, something which is 'true' not empirically but, for want of a better word, existentially. My understanding of Derrida is that he is talking about the absence of
substantive meaning, of any sort of transcendent entity, as
opposed, if you like, to transcendent nothingness, the
impossibility of filling the space implied by 'difference', the fact
that meaning always lies between words and all we can do is
chase it. This is not to do with social structures or with the
structures of action, but with life itself.

Susan Hekman introduces a different point about Giddens's
comments on Foucault (Clark *et al.* 1990). Giddens at one point
criticises Foucault for not being able to develop a critical
position, and the assumption upon which this is based is that
critical positions have to be grounded in some way in philosophy. She argues that Giddens, in making this comment, remains
trapped in an Enlightenment distinction between relative and
absolute truth and assumes that because the latter is not
established, the former is of no use. What Foucault shows,
according to Hekman, is that all judgements are historical and
contextual, and Giddens cannot grasp this. Boyne (in Bryant and
Jary 1991) makes a similar point. It seems to me that elsewhere
Giddens grasps this all too well, but that in relation to Foucault
he sheds this aspect, and it belongs in part to the same realm as
what he sheds from Derrida, something which belongs to the
ontological and existential level, an unavoidable aspect of experience which we try to cover in all sorts of ways. We cannot be
certain of anything, and especially of the most important things.
We can feel isolated from the external world, caught up in an
endless play of language, nothing which we find there seeming
to have any grip on our lives or on the external world.

One of the things that Dallmayr praises Giddens for is the
attempt to hold together the insights of post-structuralism with
those of more traditional forms of Enlightenment thought. My
argument is that Giddens fails in this task of holding together,
shedding the grasp of uncertainty, or absence that would actually

add depth to his understanding of our experience of modernity. It is, I think, extremely difficult, but also necessary, to hold both sides of this equation together. On the one hand, there is an absence of meaning, of certainty, which is terrifying and exciting at the same time (because it might mean that we can do *anything*), and on the other there is the solidity of the world, the way in which it resists us, the way in which we do actually seem to possess a knowledge of the world which enables us to do things; and there is also the experience of rational thought, the need to justify and ground our actions. All these things seem to me to be part of the human condition, but increasingly through his work Giddens sheds the internal experience, what we might call 'internal knowledge', in favour of the external. When he reaches his account of modernity, he can only deal with it as a reaction to the external world.

The other element of the experience of the modern world that Giddens sheds in his critique of structuralism in particular is the reverse side of feeling caught up in the interminable play of discourse: our experience of the world as moving inexorably onwards whatever we do, of our actions becoming the props perhaps of the very system we intend to change. We can experience ourselves in a very real sense as simply 'the bearers of social relations', puppets on invisible strings. We can contemplate the truth of the idea that agency itself, as Boyne puts it, is a myth (Bryant and Jary 1991). The nearest we get to this idea in Giddens's work is his description of modernity as a juggernaut, yet he deals with this experience as a phenomenology that does not match the reality. My argument is that there is a truth in this perception, and that structuralist analysis can capture that truth. As long as we realise that it is only part of the whole truth, then we can use it. If we fall for its proponents' claims that it is the whole truth, then we are in trouble; but so are we also if we reject it in its entirety.

Heidegger

I want to make much the same sort of point in relation to Giddens's interpretation of Heidegger; in fact, rather than work with the detail of post-structuralism I took it immediately to the realms of Heidegger's work, which, given the influence of Heidegger on Derrida, was not all that difficult to do. Heidegger, like other philosophical origins in Giddens's work, is rather like a railway station which he passed through, picking up mail on the way. In *Profiles and Critiques in Social Theory*, he describes himself as 'strongly influenced by certain aspects of Heidegger's philosophy' (Giddens 1982a: 27), and he continues to recognise this influence right through to his reply to his critics (in Held and Thompson 1989). There is, however, a considerable degree to which Heidegger's influence is replaced by that of time–geography, and I shall return to this theme in the next chapter: the existential experience of time (and space) is something else which I think Giddens leaves behind. For the moment, however, I want to concentrate on other aspects of his interpretation of Heidegger.

Heidegger's philosophy is a complex animal which can perhaps be seen from its recent history; on the one hand it has fed into existentialism with its concerns for the individual and authenticity, and on the other into post-modernism with its concerns about the constitution of the individual and, at least by implication, the impossibility of authenticity. It is the first line of interpretation that I want to look at now. The authentic individual is one who does not seek anonymity in the ontic, including socially constructed space and time, but can recognise, or experience, his or her uniqueness as an individual, and his or her orientation towards the future as full of possibilities and necessities for choice; also entailed in this is the ability to take responsibility for choice and the guilt and anxiety, or angst, which stems from choice. A vital part of one's authenticity is the recognition that one will die and the ability to care about this. It is this aspect of Heidegger's philosophy that Giddens says he does not like – it is not clear why he doesn't like it, except that he comments in *A Contemporary Critique* (1981a) that it has severe limitations from the point of view of sociological analysis.

This, of course, is not surprising since it is not intended to be a sociological analysis, which for Heidegger is confined to the ontic and is in many ways a study of the inauthentic. There is no reason why the levels of experience about which Heidegger is talking should not inform sociological analysis, which perhaps needs to recognise its complicity in the inauthentic, but Giddens is not interested in this, except, at one stage in the development of his work, for Heidegger's ideas about time and space. As a consequence this dimension is shed. That it need not be shed can be seen from a critical examination of Giddens's comment in *A Contemporary Critique* that Heidegger seems excessively influenced by Western notions of death and that:

> Where death, for example, is a transition in an external [*sic* – eternal?] cycle of rebirth, its relation to the 'authenticity' of life might be quite different from an outlook which has its roots in Judeao-Christian traditions.
>
> (Giddens 1981a: 34–5)

On one level this is quite true, and as Ernest Becker argues in *The Denial of Death* (1973), non-Western societies often have better ways of dealing with the terrible fact that each of us is going to die – ways which enable us to find some position in the universe. However, these are ways of handling the same existential fact that as human beings we all share: we are all aware of our impending death. In fact it might be possible to argue that different cosmologies enable a more authentic recognition of our death than is possible in Western societies (although I am unsure whether this would be acceptable to Heidegger), but certainly not that the ontological status of individuals in such societies is different, which is the implication of Giddens's argument.

There is, in fact, a tangle of ambiguity, if not contradictions, in Giddens's position in this area. On the one hand he rejects, or does not care about, this aspect of Heidegger's work. Yet on the other, when he comes to his own discussion of modernity, he talks about existential angst as the opposite of ontological security and a product of modernity, the loss of routine and certainty. At the very least, he could make use of existentialists' descriptions of such angst to deepen his analysis, but he does not do this. Giddens's angst is an uncertainty about one's existence produced by modern society, whereas Heidegger's is a recognition of the reality of one's existence over and against any social organisation.

Elsewhere, however, Giddens talks about an existential contradiction which he at least implies to be a trans-historical phenomenon, although it comes to the fore not in modern but in tribal societies. He seems to me to present a rather odd argument in this connection. In *The Constitution of Society* (1984) (and elsewhere) he discusses the existential contradiction of human beings as the central contradiction of tribal societies; living as they do close to nature, humans' connection to nature, as opposed to our humanness, is emphasised. Myths, he argues, mediate this contradiction on a cognitive level. As class-divided societies develop, cities become important power containers, attenuating our links with nature; the existential contradiction remains important in class-divided societies, side by side with the structural contradictions that appear with the development of the state. In class societies, structural contradictions become much more important.

Here it seems Giddens is saying, on the one hand, that living close to nature involves a consciousness of an existential contradiction, which presumably must carry a deal of angst, certainly sufficient to generate powerful mythologies to explain or contain the contradiction. On the other hand, in some of his discussions of modernity, he talks not only of the angst that seems to be a specific product of modernity, but also of the possibility that we would have a better future if we re-established something of our links with nature – even though it follows that this would bring us back into contact with our existential contradiction. In this latter view, perhaps, he is presenting an understanding of our experience of the world which is contrary to the much more intuitively acceptable view that the further we move away from nature the more acute our existential contradiction, since we lose contact with one pole of that contradiction and consequently find it harder to produce the sort of integration that perhaps myths once supplied. We become too purely human.

The overall point I want to draw from this particular discussion is that when Giddens deals with our experience of the world, he subordinates concepts appropriate to that experience – such as we can find in the work of structuralists, post-structuralists, Heidegger, and, as we shall soon see, pyschoanalysts – to sociological concepts, the concepts he develops from or builds into structuration theory. The result is an array of blunt instruments that are not adequate to grasp the complexity of experience, or its reality, and which seem to push all the time towards contradictions.

Psychoanalysis

Giddens draws at various points on Freud, Erikson and Winnicott. I want to argue that in each case he sociologises their work; I do not want to make a point about interpretation, scholarship or accuracy, but rather to extend my argument that he loses the depth of the individual and of agency.

Giddens uses Freud's work on crowd psychology to talk about regression and indentification with a leader–figure in a childlike way, tying this into his notion of ontological security; beyond this he uses the idea of the unconscious to locate motivation, although as I. Cohen (1989) points out, this account is undeveloped. My point is substantiated in the way that Giddens stresses that *he* does not believe that the unconscious intrudes into daily life except at crisis moments. The notion of the unconscious is frequently difficult to take seriously, let alone accept as part of a rational theory; Giddens seems to do this with ease, but then to deny its effect. I think from a sociologistic point of view, he is quite right to do so. If sociology is to give an account of agency and the agent, there is a sense in which it cannot allow concepts, such as the unconscious, which suggest that human beings routinely work in irrational, un-routine ways. I am suggesting, then, not only that there is a depth missing in Giddens's account of the individual, but the unitary, non-dualistic theory that he wants to develop cannot allow such a depth, which goes beyond the performance of and reaction to social practices.

In the case of Freud's work on group psychology, the complexity that is lost in Giddens's account has to do with types of identification and the complexities of projection and introjection, which, in *Central Problems in Social Theory*, he seems to lump together under the heading of 'more mature capabilities of object-choice' (Giddens 1979a: 127). My reading of Freud is that identification, even in its childlike mode, is anyway a complicated business and does not explain what Giddens wants to explain: the appearance of a powerful authority figure, or authoritarian figure, during 'critical moments'. I am quite happy to accept the notion of regression here: the emergence of authoritarian figures seems to be intimately bound up with regression, at least at one level of the personality. I am less clear whether a process of identification is involved: for Freud, identification involves wanting, consciously or unconsciously, *to be like* the figure with whom one identifies. I am not sure that it makes much sense, or explains anything, to see, for example, Germans in the 1930s and early '40s as wanting *to be like* Hitler. Would they all grow moustaches? It makes more sense to see them as wanting to be led by Hitler, as wanting the certainty that he seemed to offer, and this can be explained in psychodynamic terms by the projection of what, in the mature psyche, would be a part of the personality that could take decisions, make judgements or whatever. Crudely, it is an attempt to recreate the father figure *prior* to the identification which enables us to take over those abilities for ourselves. Rather than identifying with the authoritarian figure, we identify the authoritarian figure with an ideal parental figure (an ego-ideal), only we do so in a more intense, even desperate way than we might during normal times, when such a projection is often no more than a condition for routine group solidarity.

My point here is that the psychological processes are much more complex then Giddens allows for, and that his analysis takes away an important depth and level of understanding of agency.

Turning to Erikson's work, I have argued elsewhere (Craib 1986) that Giddens seems to reject, for example, Erikson's concept of 'ego-identity' because it embraces a number of some-times obscure internal processes, when the reality is that what it refers to *is* often obscure. In fact, Erikson gives much less weight than most to internal processes and conflicts; he is much closer to the concerns of sociology even amongst his fellow ego-psycho-logists (see Craib 1990) – yet this seems too much for Giddens. In the case of Erikson and, in *The Consequences of Modernity* (1990), the case of Winnicott, Giddens seems to turn these theorists into quasi-behaviourists and to read them as describing how the parent 'trains' the infant into a sense of ontological security through consistent and routine parenting, removing anxiety. I don't think Erikson is talking about this, and Winnicott certainly isn't. The idea of removing anxiety from a child would be, in some ways, an anathema, a prescription for bad parenting. It is more that the parent, by displaying his or her ability to hold the child's anxiety, enables the child to internalise that ability and hold – i.e. *experience* – his or her own anxiety. It is this ability and the complex internal processes that go on around it that concern Winnicott. If the well-parented person can experience anxiety, rather than avoid it, a lot of what Giddens has to say about security and routine collapses – or he has to abandon object-relations theory. In any case I will be extending this argument in the chapter on agency.

Chapter 7

The problem with structures

In this chapter I want to pursue my argument about Giddens's conception of structures, in particular in relation to ontological depth and the ontologically variegated nature of the social world. I will do so in three ways: first by looking at the 'internal' problems of conceiving of rules as structures and vice versa; secondly by collating a range of criticisms which seem to me to amount to saying that he should have a conception of structure separate from that of agency and action, re-introducing the dualism he is attempting to transcend; and finally by looking at his solution to what I will call, rather loosely, 'the problem of order', since it is often the case that theoretically the existence of social order is attached to the existence of systems or structures with emergent properties. In this last respect, I want to explore critically what he is doing with his conceptions of time and space.

Giddens presents a conception of structure as rules and resources. It is in the former of these elements, rules, that the linguistic analogy is clearly at work, and it seems to me unavoidable that this should be the case, not only because of the pervasiveness of the 'linguistic turn' in twentieth-century theory, which makes such an analogy hard to avoid, but also because language as a system of rules presents such a neat model for some of the things that sociologists want to talk about. In Giddens's work, we might say that the analogy becomes reality, insofar as, according to his concept, the structures of action share some of the properties of the structures of language, and, of course, reflexive, discursive consciousness plays such a large part in his theory of action. I think that several critics, including my slightly younger self, have misunderstood this, reading Giddens as if he were developing a concept theoretically equivalent to Parsons' system or to Marxist or Weberian ideas of social structure. In fact this is not the case – his concept of 'system' is the nearest we come to such conventional ideas of structure. It seems rather pointless to criticise something for not being what it doesn't try to be. Hence my distinction between 'internal' criticisms of his concept of structure – largely having to do with the nature of rules – and those criticisms that say, in effect, that we still need a more, traditional conception of structure because it helps to explain things that otherwise can't be explained.

A lot seems to hinge on the ontological status we give to structures in Giddens's sense. As we have seen, Giddens talks about them having a 'virtual' existence, outside of time and space; William Outhwaite (in Clark *et al.* 1990) uses Bhaskar's transcendental realism to suggest that we should nevertheless grant them an ontological status, Giddens's rules having similar qualities to Bhaskar's societies. He points to Giddens's statements about rules existing in 'memory traces'. It seems to me, however, not simply a matter of saying that something exists, but also of how it exists and that, intuitively, rules – whether or not they exist in memory traces – have a different form of existence to families, universities, social classes, modes of production or whatever. I will return to this later; for the moment I simply want to note it as my justification for dividing my discussion.

STRUCTURES AS RULES AND RESOURCES

The most systematic treatment of this issue that I have found is in a paper by J. B. Thompson (In Held and Thompson 1989). Thompson recognises the novelty of Giddens's conception of structure, but argues that it obscures more than it illuminates. He asks the very simple question: what are the rules which constitute social structure? How do we sort them out from others – presumably not all rules are of equal status. Giddens distinguishes between normative rules and semantic rules, and all rules relate both to the constitution of meaning and the sanctioning of conduct; when he develops his example of the mathematical rule (of how to progress in a series), is this meant to apply to all rules or those rules other than semantic and normative rules? Thompson makes these points, he says, to show the looseness of

Giddens's concept of structure, but I think it goes beyond this to show the looseness of the concept of rule per se. This is not meant to be a criticism of any use of the concept of rule – language, after all, seems infinite in its subtlety, and the notion of rules is a helpful one precisely because of its looseness. What I am not sure about is whether such a looseness is appropriate when talking about social structures.

Thompson clearly thinks it is not. He argues that the study of rules is actually something clear and distinct from the study of social structure. We need to distinguish which rules are important for social structure, and we can only do so by treating the two as separate. To offer my own example, the laws enshrining rights to private property are clearly more important than the rule which tells me to take my medicine three times a day: yet the only way we can establish that importance is through an implicit or explicit reference to a concept of social structure, which would change more radically if laws relating to private property were abolished than if I forgot to take my medicine. Thompson offers some more precise examples. If we study the use of the term *left* in British politics, we look at the semantic structure of English, but simply by doing this we do not analyse the social structure – we do that by showing how rules are differentiated according to sex, class, etc., which we have to assume exist separately from rules.

Thompson then goes on to discuss Giddens's distinctions between structural principles, structural sets and axes of structuration. I am quoting the following passage in full because I think it is much clearer than any summary I could produce:

A structural principle, such as that which 'operates along an axis' relating urban areas to rural hinterlands, is not a 'rule' in any ordinary sense: it is neither a semantic rule, nor a moral rule, nor a 'formula' which expresses what actors know in knowing how to go in social life. To insist that a structural principle '*must*' be some such rule, or must be capable of being analysed in terms of rules, is to force on the material a mode of conceptualisation which is not appropriate to it, and which stems less from a reflection upon the structural features of social life than from an implicit ontology of structure. Similarly it seems unhelpful and misleading to interpret Marx's account of structural relations involved in the capitalist system of production in terms of 'sets of rules and resources'. The constitution of labour power as a commodity, the determination of its value as the labour time socially necessary for its production . . . these features of the capitalist system cannot be treated as so many 'rules' which the workers follow when they turn up at the factory gates. . . .

(in Held and Thompson 1989: 68–9)

This is reinforced by the point that it is quite possible to transform an institution (in the conventional, non-Giddens sense), like a factory, without transforming the structural relations that make it a capitalist factory.

Giddens's replies to these points represent for me one of the most difficult parts of his whole work; one response I have is that I simply do not understand it (and it is of some comfort to note that Albrow (1990) has also commented on its frustrating nature). It is almost as if Giddens has a blind spot here; he cannot see what is being got at. He makes it clear that his concept of structure is novel, and that he is trying to move away from the notion of structure as something external to agency, but he does not seem to realise that this is precisely what is being criticised. So it is wrong, he argues, *given his definition of structure*, to ask which rules make up social structure. Of course it is wrong, but it is his definition of structure which is being criticised precisely because this question cannot be asked. In one of his more arcane formulations, he repeats his definition of structure:

In my usage, structure is what gives *form* and *shape* to social life, but is not *itself* that form and shape – nor should 'give' be understood in an active sense here, because structure only exists in and through the activities of human agents.

(Giddens 1989b: 256)

This takes us so far away from any traditional notion of structure, so clearly into properties of action, that it leaves us with nothing to say about social organisation at all. It becomes a precondition of social organisation, of social systems or social structures, but no more than that. It is on a par with saying that human beings are rational, or are users of symbols. Yet in the main body of his work, Giddens clearly wants the concept of structure to do much more work than this. This quotation also demonstrates the vicious circle pointed out by Smith and Turner (1986): that agency presupposes structure and structure presupposes agency.

In relation to Thompson's point about the analysis of the term *left*, Giddens suggests that the semantic analysis of the term's use could lead us towards understanding several aspects of the reproduction of organisations and of power differentials; the use of the term is constitutive of what it identifies. This is true, and I imagine would be acceptable to Thompson, but it seems to miss the latter's point – that the analysis itself depends upon a prior and implicit conception of social structure that Giddens's theory cannot recognise. Again there is a vicious circle: Giddens suggests a way of analysing social structures which actually depends on those structures already having been analysed.

Finally, Giddens accepts Thompson's point that a structural principle cannot be seen as a rule, and denies that he has ever suggested that it could. Instead, a structural principle deals with aspects of social systems, connected with institutional orderings and time–space distantiation. Again this seems to me true, but it points to a dramatic change in his use of the concept of structure that has nothing to do with the original definition. If structures are rules and resources, then why use the term *structural principle* to refer to something that has nothing to do with rules?

I think that what is happening here is that Giddens is using *structure* in structural principle (and structural sets, etc.) in a sense much closer to its traditional one, and it emphasises Thompson's point about an implicit (and I think conventional, in a common-sense way) idea of structure which underlies a lot of his arguments. It is most apparent in the contradiction noted by Perry Anderson (1990) that Giddens's theory is eminently voluntaristic (some critics argue only voluntaristic), yet his historical analyses point to the dominance of system tendencies against our ability to change the world. In the former, we find his explicit conception of structure; in the latter his implicit conception is at work.

STRUCTURE AS SOCIAL STRUCTURE

Giddens does not attribute to systems qualities that have conventionally been attributed to structures, although implicitly in his historical accounts, and especially in his account of modernity, systems have the objectivity and the power more usually attributed to structures. In this section I want to survey a range of criticisms about structuration theory that point to this

absence and to develop my earlier arguments that there is a range
of phenomena that structuration theory excludes from consideration and that we need in order to think about social structures as
possessing a real existence, a 'depth existence' in the social world,
different from the existence of rules, agents and agency.

(1) My first point comes from papers by Derek Layder (1981)
and Margaret Archer (1982; and in Clark *et al.* 1990) and has to do
with whether structuration theory enables us to grasp the complexity of the relationship between freedom and determination in
human life. Layder points out that Giddens seems to see the only
alternative to structuration theory as a thoroughgoing structural
determinism. Either people produce structures or are produced
by them. It seems to me that both of these statements may be true
at the same time, if in different ways.

Both freedom and determination are complex ideas, and the
two can be inextricably linked, in experience, in the inner world,
and in the external social world. For example, Giddens sees our
reflexive ability as an important part of the control we have over
the social world. That is certainly true: in our individual and
social worlds, we can look around us, identify what is going on
and institute changes – some of the time. Some of the time we can
look around us, identify what is going on and find ourselves
incapable of instituting changes. That is as true for my grasp of
the way my behaviour is endangering my marriage as it is for my
inability to effect the growth of multi-national corporations.
Sometimes our capacity for reflective thought can leave us
recognising but unable to do anything about our lack of freedom.
Sometimes, in our personal relationships, our freedom lies in
following, being determined by, our instincts. And, of course,
determination can mean several things: an inevitable, billiard-
ball-like chain reaction, where there is no alternative (and I
would agree with Giddens that such a conception is not much
use in the social sciences); or it could mean a much more
complex process framing causal mechanisms which limit
outcomes without making one particular outcome inevitable –
an idea which is much more appropriate to sociology. My
proposition is that there is much more at work here than
unintended consequences or limits on the extent to which
discursive knowledge can penetrate the social world, which is
how I imagine Giddens would deal with these issues.

Archer argues that Giddens does not provide us with any way

of looking at degrees of freedom and restraint. In the case of restraint, she points out that, at any one time, certain structural properties are more amenable to change than others. My own example would be that it is easier to change the assessment rules for my students' essays than it is to replace the English language with Esperanto. Giddens's theory, however, suggests no way in which we can make those distinctions, which have to do with freedom and constraint. My main point here is that to make such distinctions, we need to conceive of agency and structure as separate: it is only if they are seen as two sides of the same coin that we have to choose between freedom and determination.

(2) Archer and Nicos Mouzelis (1989) argue that there are occasions when we have to treat structure and agency as at least analytically distinct if we are going to gain a purchase on certain important problems. For Archer, it is necessary to make this separation to study the relationship of agency and structure over time – we have to identify structures which are acted upon by agents. In a similar vein, Mouzelis argues that the idea of structuration does not cover all the possible relationships between actors on the one hand and rules and resources on the other. It deals with what he calls the natural/performative relationship using first-order concepts, by which I take him to mean it deals with, or describes what we are doing in, our immediate, everyday lives – when we are just getting on with things and not thinking about them too much. In that situation, we are producing, reproducing and transforming structures, and there is a 'duality' of structure. When we take a theoretical attitude, however, there is a *dualism*: we are looking at and dealing with structures as external features of the world. He makes the point that such a change in orientation also often involves a change from individual to collective actors, and several commentators have referred to Giddens's difficulty in dealing with the latter. Neither Giddens's historical sociology nor the emphasis he places on reflexive monitoring grasp this implication of a dualism, although it is there in his work.

This point also backs up a point Archer makes about the nature of constraint: that when we are trying to change something, when, in other words, there is a dualism, the constraint exercised by the structure cannot be assumed to be insignificant:

Nations can fall, polities be deposed and economies

> bankrupted while efforts are being made to change the factors
> responsible. As a general theoretical proposition, this holds
> good, however short the time interval involved. Yet this is
> what Giddens spirits away by making structural properties
> atemporal, and according them only a pale 'virtual existence'
> (in Clark *et al.* 1990, p. 79)

I will return to the issue of constraint shortly; the point I want to
make here is that a clear case can be made not only that there is a
dualism, an opposition of actors and structure in such situations,
but also that the relationship varies according to the nature of the
structure we are dealing with. This is sometimes a matter of scale:
nations do not fall while I try to change assessment rules (except
coincidentally), whereas nation after nation has fallen whilst
people have tried to change capitalism, not just coincidentally.
More important however, it is a different thing to reflect on and
try to change, for example, sexual rules (from, perhaps, 'condoms
spoil the fun' to 'condoms keep us alive') than to change the laws
of inheritance relating to illegitimate children or to change
capitalism. We are dealing with different types of object, and this
calls for different forms of understanding and different forms of
action. We are dealing with structures of thought and action in
one case, with legal structures in the next, and with social
structures in the third; it does not help matters to group them all
together as *social* structures, or as *structures*; and at least for the
period when we are reflecting on and trying to change them, we
can regard them as having an external existence.

(3) Derek Layder (1981) and John Urry (1982) both raise the
question of the nature of the 'virtual existence' of rules: can they
(or, I suppose, can *anything* that is outside time and space) have
an existence? On the whole, I am happy to accept this way of
describing *certain* sorts of rules, of which we are only implicitly
aware, at least until we do become aware of them and try to
formulate them, and study them in their 'instantiation': then it
seems to me they do have a real existence outside of ourselves, and
that would follow from the above argument. William Outhwaite
(in Clark *et al.* 1990) makes a case, using Bhaskar's work, that we
can treat Giddens's conception of structure as implying that
structures have a real existence, although I am by no means sure
that Giddens means them to be taken in this way. If they have a
real existence, then it does not help to say that their existence is

'virtual' and if they are real, we must be able to distinguish them from agency, on which they might none the less be dependent. Urry goes on to make the point that Giddens does not explain how structures come to be realised in systems. In fact, it seems to me that Giddens's answer on an ontological level is simply 'through agency', but this does not enable us to study the process. Giddens (1982b) recognises the force of Urry's comment but does not consider that it really affects his theory.

This emphasises the peculiarity of the ontological status he gives to structures. Urry argues that either structures appear in systems in what he calls an 'essentialist' way (I imagine him to mean by this that structures appear everywhere, rather like God is everywhere), or the number of empirical mediations are so great that it becomes impossible to study structures. My interpretation of this is that Urry is suggesting that if empirical reality is so complex in its mediation, either we have to accept the existence of structures on faith or abandon the idea. It seems to me quite appropriate to say we can only have faith in, but not know, something which has only a virtual existence, but it is not a very firm basis for a social theory.

(4) Next, I want to turn to the issue of structural constraints and a debate between Giddens and J. B. Thompson (in Held and Thompson 1989). Thompson makes many of the points I have already touched on, including Giddens's difficulty in talking about different degrees of constraint and freedom, which, I argued, can only properly be grasped by conceiving of two complex structures – agents or agency and social structures – which are separate and different but mutually dependent. By combining them together in a concept of structuration, Giddens loses something important.

One thing that happens is that when he discusses freedom he confuses a concept of freedom which is appropriate to agency and a concept that is appropriate to the relationship between agency and structure. One point which Thompson makes is that Giddens defines the agent in such a way that he or she cannot *not* be free. Giddens in his reply re-asserts this, making his usual contrast between complete determinism and complete freedom. On the one hand I am happy to accept this. I have a choice about the way in which I go to my execution, whether I starve with dignity, how I deal with a life sentence. To use Giddens's own example, it is only when I am drugged and forcibly moved by others that I have no such choice. This is my psychic freedom, my responsibility for myself, my actions and my feelings.

However, there are other freedoms: Do I have an opportunity to vote for my government? Do I have a wide or narrow range of jobs from which to choose? If I want to work, do I have to work in a job where wages keep me on or below a poverty line? These choices are not always my responsibility. They result from something we can call 'social structure', and the experience we have of these structures is often similar to that we have of the physical world, the constraints of which Giddens *can* recognise. Thompson repeats the argument I mentioned earlier, that to understand *these* restraints as they exist, for example, in capitalist societies requires a description of a system that cannot be dealt with simply in terms of rules and resources. In response, Giddens repeats his conception of structural constraint:

> Structural constraint derives from the institutionalised nature of social practices in a given context of action in which an agent finds himself or herself. Examining the nature of institutionalisation is inseparable from analysing the recursive characteristics of structure, but the constraining elements themselves have to be seen as expressing the 'given-ness' of the social environment of action to particular agents.
>
> (Giddens 1989b: 258)

To say that certain practices are institutionalised does not respond to Thompson's point that the constraining features of the capitalist system cannot be understood through the idea of rules, nor, presumably, through a concept of institutionalisation. It is simply an assertion of disagreement. But there is a more interesting phrase here, which crops up several times in Giddens's writings, about the way in which systems or institutions are 'given' to individuals. To individuals (and perhaps to groups?), then, institutions appear given, possibly immutable, as perhaps even 'external', but somehow they are not really so. Is that because they are the creation of some other individuals and groups about whom the first lot don't know? No, except perhaps in some distant historical sense that they were once produced by somebody, since they pre-exist existing individuals and presumably will survive them. Yet at the same time they are produced and maintained by all existing individuals, so presumably they could be changed by all existing individuals. I must admit that I get lost in all the implications of this, and it might be that I am simply misunderstanding Giddens. None the less, it does seem that he is rather desperately defending his ontology of praxis, since if institutions pre-date and survive their actors, what is there to distinguish them from social structures in the more conventional sense?

I want now to draw the discussion in this section to a conclusion. I have picked out a range of points from critical reactions to Giddens's notion of structure and argued that they point in the direction of separating agency and structure in the conventional way and that such separation does not imply, as Giddens seems to believe, that we must adopt a thoroughgoing determinism. There is a strong case to be made that the qualities that are conventionally attributed to social structure by sociologists are important and that Giddens offers no alternative. We need make no decision about which of the available, more conventional candidates is better. Three emerge quite clearly from the critical literature. Margaret Archer (1982) juxtaposes to Giddens a morphogenetic approach (Buckley 1967 and 1968; Maruyama 1963) which originates from within general systems theory and which allows for emergent properties in systems and focuses attention on interchanges across boundaries; there is the Marxist notion of underlying structures that is in Bhaskar's work and is elaborated on in Layder's discussions (1981 and 1985); and there is a modified functionalism.

I do not intend to rule out Giddens's conception of structure. It seems to me that it works best with those aspects of social action which are closest to language: the rules which govern routine everyday interactions, and perhaps especially those belonging to the realm of practical consciousness. Thompson points out that one of Giddens's main contributions has been to bring the sociologists of action, Garfinkel, the phenomenologists, and Goffman into the fold of a general sociology. My argument is that we still need more traditional conceptions.

THE PROBLEM OF ORDER

There are various ways of approaching the 'problem of order' in sociology, all of which involve the problem of moving from individual action and interaction through to societies or social systems; I want to approach it in the most general sense, posed by

Jeffrey Alexander (1985), of the way in which we understand the existence of non-random patterns in social life. For the morphogenetic approach, and for Marxism, this is barely a problem: the system or the structure is the starting point of analysis and the non-random patterns that we can discover can be understood in terms of the properties of the system or structure. For Giddens, however, given that his starting point is praxis, agency and individual agents, it is much more of a problem. There are at least five answers in his work, and there is no reason to suppose that he would not argue that they all contribute to social order. I will deal with each in turn: structures; routine practices; unintended consequences; reflexive monitoring; and the time-space constitution of social systems, giving most space to the last.

Before going on to these issues, however, I want to make some general points about the issue of social order. There are questions that regularly appear in sociology that I suspect are rather like questions about the meaning of life. It is unlikely that we will ever find an answer. One response is simply to get on with it and enjoy ourselves, but questions about meaning have a tendency to intrude; we can never simply be, like inanimate objects, or allow ourselves to be subjected to a regular, repetitive life cycle, like plants. That is, perhaps, part of the misfortune of being human. So, at least periodically and for the more neurotic amongst us, a great deal of the time, questions about meaning become important. In these situations, it is less the possibility of answers that makes speculation interesting than the development of metaphors for understanding where we are and what we are doing, finding new and perhaps more useful ways of thinking about the world.

I suspect that questions about the problem of order are like this. For many sociologists, for a lot of the time, the problem of order is not a problem – the questions of research are concrete and interesting and sufficient. However, for some people – and perhaps some of the time for all people – the question intrudes, and sometimes the answers are useful, even if they are metaphors, and can provide guides to research. This seems to be how Giddens sometimes regards not only his responses to the problem of order but his theory as a whole. The same points could be made about the various other ontologies of social life that co-exist in sociology.

There are times, however, when Giddens seems to be claiming

to put forward answers to the 'problem of order'. My following points should be taken in this context. The 'solutions' that emerge from Giddens's work might very well be interesting and point to research; my argument is basically that they should not be taken as answers. One of his answers in particular, unintended consequences, is, I think, a basis for further speculation which provides a further justification for allowing, in addition to Giddens's notion of structure, another notion which sees structures as having a real, external existence and a determining effect, which might on occasion come close to a mechanistic causality.

Structure

I have already quoted Giddens's statement that structure gives form and shape to social life, without itself being that form and shape. If we attribute to structures alone the role of producing non-random patterns of interaction through the medium of praxis, and give those structures a 'virtual' existence, then I think we are, as Urry points out, in the realms of essentialism (Urry 1982). *Essentialism* is often used in sociology as a dirty word, but here I think its use has some validity. Simply taken by itself, structure – or structuring properties or whatever – seems to be a magical property that agency somehow possesses and passes on. Giddens does not elaborate on empirical mediations but does assign a role to agency in instantiating structures, and this leads us on to the place he gives routine and, through routine, ontological security. By itself, structure is the least adequate understanding of social order on offer in his work.

Routine practices

In his early work, routine is the major source of patterning, producing the most deeply embedded institutions of social life and social systems. Routine rests upon ontological security, and in this sense social order is rooted in the personality structure: we have a need for routine, we develop routine practices and pass them on from generation to generation less through direct socialisation than through the 'hidden curriculum' where we learn what to do by learning the implicit rules of how to go on. In *Central Problems in Social Theory*, he writes:

> Ontological security can be taken to depend upon the implicit faith actors have in the conventions (codes of signification and forms or normative regulation) via which the duality of structure, the reproduction of social life is effected. In most circumstances of social life, the sense of ontological security is routinely grounded in mutual knowledge employed such that the interaction is 'unproblematic' or can be largely 'taken for granted'.
>
> (Giddens 1979a: 219)

I used this quotation in my earlier paper (Craib 1986) and I still agree with the point I made there. Comparing Giddens to Parsons, I argued that the former is producing a view of social order very much like that of the latter, but reversing the order of priority between individual and system. For Parsons, the stable personality is the product of the social system that is working well; for Giddens the social order, the social system, is the product of a stable personality working routinely. Social order exists because we are creatures of habit.

I will be arguing against Giddens's conception of the personality in the next chapter; for the moment I will confine myself to pointing out the inadequacies of this as a basis for understanding the existence of social order. It is in this part of his work that he comes closest to the sociology of Garfinkel (1967), for whom it is actually not the social order itself but our sense of social order which is the product of constant work on the part of those involved in interaction. It seems to me that Garfinkel's position is more credible: he is talking about the construction of meaning – in this case the meaning we give to 'social system' or 'institution' – and clearly this is an ongoing process of construction using, amongst other things, all the implicit rules of practical consciousness that form the object of his work. Giddens, however, is not talking about the routine ways in which we construct meanings, but the routine ways in which we construct the 'real thing', institutions and social systems themselves. My objection to this idea is that institutions and social systems are actually much more complicated animals than simple routines. They are often, if not always, the sites for contradiction, for more or less radical change and, in the case of modernity, for the systematic questioning and transformation of routines. Giddens recognises all this, most clearly in the *The Consequences of Modernity* (1990), and it seems from this book in particular, but also generally whenever he approaches the analysis of the modern world, that routine cannot be the basis of the social order. In fact, increasingly it seems to be relegated to being of primary importance in traditional societies, as once having been the basis for social order.

Unintended consequences and reflexive monitoring

In their introduction to a paper by Giddens on structuration theory, Knorr-Cetina and Cicourel (1981) note the importance of the concept of unintended consequences in moving us from the analysis of interaction, from micro-sociology, to the analysis of systems, macro-sociology. When Giddens talks about homeostatic loops as a mode of system regulation, these are produced by the unintended consequences of action, which in turn become the unacknowledged conditions of future action.

What is interesting to me about this suggestion is that there is no a priori reason why unintended consequences should take the form of regular patterning. In fact it seems to me that the phrase 'unintended consequences' simply poses the problem: we might be able to trace through those consequences and provide an historical explanation, which is what Giddens intends, but to say that something did happen is not the same as saying why that thing happened – why should unintended consequences add to or create a patterned system? It could be because we are rational beings, and our actions interlock in a more or less rational way, even though we are not aware of the processes involved. That answer is perhaps the answer implied by being directed to give an historical account of the processes involved. It would be sufficient, and perhaps is sufficient, I think, if we are dealing only with more or less direct relationships between people; we can understand family dynamics, for example, in terms of the conscious and, more importantly, unconscious (unintended, unacknowledged) reactions of members to each other, and show how these reactions create a pattern which might or might not be productive for its members. These patterns can be traced, understood and reflexively monitored, and perhaps changed. Giddens's way of approaching unintended consequences and the role he gives to reflexive monitoring seems to me appropriate in this sort of example. We begin by attributing the patterned nature of family interaction to unintended consequences and end by attributing it to reflexive monitoring.

But when we are talking about large-scale systems, institutions, or societies, something else is going on. All these social relationships are mediated not just by members' interaction but by the relationship of all members to the physical world. Giddens gives very little prominence to the physical world; he recognises that it has a constraining effect (we cannot, at the moment at any rate, grow corn in the desert) but beyond that he is wary of it. I suspect this is part and parcel of his rejection of evolutionary theory, with the idea of societies adapting to their environment.

It is possible, however, to give a rather different role to the physical world in the organisation of social life. To show this, I want to turn to the work of Jean-Paul Sartre, particularly his *The Critique of Dialectical Reason* (1976). Sartre too is presenting an ontology of social life, although his ontology is intended to criticise and to provide a basis for Marxism. He develops in particular a concept of the 'practico-inert', a 'humanised' physical world, humanised not by incorporation into human life through rules but by physical labour, bringing about the physical transformation of that world. The physical world in this conception is not a brute existent, a limit and setting for human activity, nor is it something defined in and by human consciousness and action; it is a result of the interactions between the two.

Physical labour has consequences. Some of these clearly stem from the actions, knowledge, intentions of human beings, but some clearly stem from natural laws, the natural, physical processes which we might or might not understand. The practico-inert is a combination of these; the physical world takes on some of the aspects of human action – it 'does things' to people – whilst human action takes on some of the 'weight' of the physical world, becomes subjected to and incorporated into the laws of nature. Perhaps an example taken from Sartre will show this more clearly: Chinese peasants each individually, separately and perhaps competitively extended their arable land by cutting through forests in the northern part of the country. The result is that they removed a natural flood barrier and laid open their communities to 'natural' disaster. Thus many separate, individual activities became united, drawn together by the natural world, and the people found their activity, which we can regard as rational given a certain state of knowledge, turned against them as the threat, and then reality, of systematic destruction, which finally drove them from the land.

This example is apposite given the current concern with world-wide eco-disaster – a threat which Giddens recognises clearly in *The Consequences of Modernity* (1990) and elsewhere. My purposes in using it here are more abstract, and perhaps trivial in the face of the reality. What it shows for theory is the way human action and the laws of nature combine in a systematic way such that the physical world *and* human society are transformed; the physical is also a medium for human relationships and adds to human relationships some of its law-governed, determined processes. This provides a foundation for conceiving of social structures in a different way to Giddens and in a way that he rejects, yet it can be developed from the importance he gives unintended consequences, as a way of making sense of the systematic nature of what is unintended.

Time and space

As his work progresses, Giddens comes to give immense weight to the issues of time and space. In the *Constitution of Society* (1984), he locates time and space at the centre of the problem of order, and the problem of order at the centre of social theory:

> The fundamental question of social theory as I see it – the 'problem of order' conceived of in a way quite alien to Parsons' formulation – is to explicate how the limitations of individual 'presence' are transcended by the 'stretching' of social relations across time and space.
>
> (Giddens 1984: 38)

Understanding what Giddens has to say about time and space has presented me with considerable problems. I am often not quite sure what he is trying to say, but I *think* I may have at least discovered the source of my confusion. Sometimes, he seems to be offering a *description* of social systems in terms of their organisation of time and space; sometimes he seems to be offering a meta-theory of time and space, which are seen as constituting societies, an explanation of social order, rather than a way of posing the problem of social order. The former attempt seems to me much more useful than the latter, and the confusion arises when he runs them together. Thus Peter Saunders argues (in Held and Thompson 1989) that there can be no such thing as a meta-theory of time and space, drawing on Giddens's meta-theoretical statements. Giddens's reaction is to agree with Saunders' conclusion, drawing on his own descriptive statements.

The idea that Giddens is presenting a theory of time and space comes with his introduction of the issues through the work of Heidegger. There is, I think, a real sense in which Heidegger does present such a theory, and he does give time a constitutive role on an ontological level. When we talk about the social organisation of time, whether in traditional or modern societies, however, we have moved away from ontology, and to talk of time (and space) as constitutive of social systems is merely to say that time and space are aspects of social systems, and in fact that different social systems organise time and space in different ways. Most of Giddens's discussion of time–space distantiation is about the way in which systems – or perhaps more accurately in terms of structuration theory, the practices that constitute systems – organise time and space. To move from the ontological to the ontic level is to give the 'doing' role to social practices, not to time as part of *dasein*.

If I am right, however, and Giddens uses time and space as general descriptive criteria of comparing, often instructively, different types of social system, then its relation to the problem of order becomes rather obscure. Cohen (in Clark *et al.* 1990) follows Giddens in talking about the way time–geography can build time–space models, what he calls time–space morphology, the study of forms. In the same collection, Stinchcombe points out that this is not a new way of posing the problem of order – Gerth and Mills (1953) posed it in the same way nearly forty years ago. In fact, a regular response to Giddens is that sociology has taken time and space more seriously than he contends. Stinchcombe goes on to give an account of what Giddens is getting at that I find clearer than Giddens himself, and which I will quote at some length:

> [T]he most strategic way to describe institutions and their moral evolution is to trace how they define and regulate situations defined by temporal and spatial boundaries . . . and

then to trace out the relations these bear to the schedules of movements of people from and to situations defined and controlled by other institutions. . . . What has an institutional role is not the individual but the time–space unit, the situation of co-presence. What people know is not how to play a role, but how to respond to and learn the praxis of a situation. People change roles, either in the course of their daily movement or in the course of making institutionally consequential choices in their own lives, by choosing to move into (or by being coerced into) a given sort of situation. The basic units of social structure for Giddens are not an individual's statuses and roles, as we have been taught to think, but situations with defined praxes, which we move into and out of and have our current behaviour shaped by. Institutionalised situations with their moral and practical arrangements create individuals' obligations and powers, create activities, so they and not the roles are causally significant.

(in Clark *et al.* 1990: 50)

This summary brings to light both the good points and the difficulties and contradictions in Giddens's conception of time-space. I think that Stinchcombe shows how this way of looking at the social world goes beyond role theory and incorporates the insights of a range of theories from ethnomethodology to time-geography. At the same time, I think, it would be wrong to take it as a radical rejection of role-theory – in content, I am not sure there is all that much difference between the idea of learning a role and that of learning 'the praxis of a situation', except that calling it the latter extends the ideas we can bring into it; it also loses something – the implication of *role playing*, of there being something about everyday life of *acting*, is lost, for example. Giddens argues explicitly against interpretations of Goffman that bring this idea to the fore, but I shall argue in the next chapter that this dimension is true to our experience of social life and thus important.

The more general problems that emerge in this paragraph are those picked out by Gregor McLennan (in Clark *et al.* 1990). The first is the difficulty of avoiding an ontic, everyday conception of time and space, basically clock-time and measured space, of which Giddens is so critical when he writes on the theory of space-time. The analysis of institutions is and must be based on socially constructed time and space, and I think the socially constructed time and space of our society, even when we are talking about very different societies. It is only in comparison with our measured time and space that other conceptions begin to emerge. We can only understand what Giddens calls reversible time (the time of traditional societies engaged in cycles connected with nature) by comparison with our own conception of time. Once this is seen, it becomes easier to understand McLennan's point that we cannot avoid doing another thing that Giddens warns against: conceiving of time in 'spatial' terms and conceiving of both as an environment in which things happen. This is certainly the dominant conception in Stinchcombe's account. It seems that when Giddens is writing about the theory of time and space, the insights cannot be translated into analysis, and McLennan's comments about another aspect of Giddens's philosophical awareness and its application to social theory apply here as well:

> Better perhaps to leave the philosophy of internal time-consciousness to phenomenology, and the empirical scaling of the well-trodden pathways from home to school and back to time-geography.
>
> (in Clark *et al.* 1990: 136)

Another way of putting this is that Giddens falls between two stools: the ontological and the ontic, with the result that the significance of the former is lost and, if we take John Urry's discussion of his ontic analysis seriously (in Bryant and Jary 1991), the latter is not explored in sufficient depth.

A further point is that not only do we tend to revert back to seeing time and space as environments in which things happen, agency moves away from agents and towards something else: institutions, social systems, practices, etc. The actors in the various time–space slots become as much subjected to praxis and its rules as, in functionalist theory, they become subjected to roles. Time and space become not in themselves *constitutive* of social life but constituted by institutions and practices as the site of activities. This in fact moves the problem of order away from time–space organisation (which is simply another phrase for the problem of order) and towards structure, routine practices, etc.

CONCLUSION

My main point in this section has been that it is perhaps easier to conceive of there being patterned relationships in society if we conceive of social systems possessing emergent properties, or of underlying social structures with a real external existence, or perhaps both, in addition to Giddens's conceptions of rules and practices. The problem of order in fact disappears – it is no longer something we have to explain but something the existence of which we can take for granted, and so get on with the job of analysing its nature and mechanisms. This is in fact what most empirical sociologists do most of the time. Wisely. I have tried to indicate that the features to which Giddens attributes social order are not sufficient by themselves to carry that weight, although on probing they perhaps reveal the case for attributing social order elsewhere.

Chapter 8

The problem with people

Turning now to the issue of agency, the social actor and the person, once again part of my aim will be to try to show that Giddens loses important dimensions in these areas, and that these lost dimensions point not only to the existence of external social structures but also to the existence of internal psychological structures of much more complexity and ambiguity and to more complex relationships between the two than is allowed for in structuration theory. Of all his work, it is, for me, his view of the personality which leaves most to be desired and adds least to the armoury of sociology.

ACTION

Giddens argues that he uses the term praxis for its implication of the transformative qualities of action. It is a term more usually associated with Marxist philosophy, emphasising the way in which people act to change their world, and it includes, for most Marxists quite centrally, the idea of labour, of work in the physical world. The term praxis, and the centrality of labour, is lost in the work of the interpretive sociologists. Insofar as they have pretensions to presenting a general social theory, this has always puzzled me, since labour seems such a clear and necessary part of human life, and there seems no good reason for absorbing it into our perceptions and conceptions, which is what usually happens. In Giddens's work, this absorption seems tied up with his fear that any sort of determinism means an absolute determinism and with his rejection of the evolutionary idea of adaptation; thus if we see human society as having to deal with the requirements of production, we have to see it as determined and possibly evolving in relation to the outside world. The transformative power of action, of praxis, thus seems to lose the material dimension involved in labour, a point I have made in a different context in relation to the work of Sartre.

Yet at the same time Giddens occasionally calls his theory a realist one, and he acknowledges the constraining qualities of the body as physical limits. Yet one could, and some do, argue that the body and its constraints are social constructions, the result of our employment of the implicit and explicit rules of social life. Giddens certainly takes this view of the resources which make up structures – they become resources through rules, so it seems inconsistent to exclude the body. When he talks about constraints in *The Constitution of Society*, he attributes the physical environment with a similar constraining quality; it becomes a brute force, as it were, at the edges of society, not as something which enters into the centre of our being. Taking this into account, and taking labour into account, does not necessarily, it seems to me, lead to a Marxist position, although it would lead to a position that I suspect Giddens would not like. But once again there is a dimension of analysis that is lost: his conception of action, of praxis, is taken from one limited, although dominant, area of modern philosophy, and the sort of foundational analysis we can find in Marxism or classic philosophy is rejected; the result, as I shall argue in the next chapter, is that Giddens gets caught up in what might be called the 'philosophical ideology' of modernism. He is caught in the linguistic turn.

THE SOCIAL ACTOR

I am using the term *actor* quite deliberately for the connotations I mentioned at the end of the last chapter. By way of leading into my arguments about his view of the personality, I want to look at Giddens's treatment of the work of Goffman, and in particular his defence of certain aspects of Goffman's work. Goffman, it has been argued – particularly by Gouldner (1970) – presents a view of the individual appropriate to late capitalism, especially in its North American manifestations. The individual becomes *only* an actor, moving from role to role, engaging in the behaviour which will best 'sell' him- or herself, and avoiding slips, fissures in the performance. On the whole, I find this a fair point about

Goffman's studies that can best be seen in terms of *role*. It is not fair or relevant to a book such as *Frame Analysis* (Goffman 1974), Giddens's interpretation of which is, rightly I think, that Goffman is describing the implicit rules of interaction, the manifestations of 'practical consciousness'.

It is, however, role-theory that I am primarily concerned with here. Role-theory has always had a tendency towards social determinism, especially as it was taken up in Parsons' work. A status role is a social position with certain expectations attached to it, expectations the individual learns on entering the role and internalises. The simplest form of the theory argues that meeting these internalised expectations becomes tied up with the identity of the individual in the role. We thus become socialised, as simply as that. More elaborate forms of the theory talk about 'role-making' as well as 'role-taking', arguing that, for example, roles are moulded by the individual to create some sort of consistency in identity from situation to situation. The conception of identity, of the non-socialised part of the self – G. H. Mead's 'I' – has always been problematic, and Goffman comes close to disposing of it altogether. He makes the occasional gesture in the direction of identity, and in his defence Giddens quotes (Giddens 1987a: 118) Goffman's comments from (interestingly enough) *Frame Analysis* (Goffman 1974) about the existence of a 'perduring moral character . . . animal nature and so forth'. This is not exactly a theory of the self or the personality or identity, and it is difficult to see, given Goffman's concentration on micro-situations and the way we fit into them, where a 'perduring moral character' might come from.

It is, I think, fairly easy to see how this emphasis on the maintenance of role rather than identity – the emphasis, in fact, on 'how people go on' in situations, as opposed on the what it is that goes on – moves into the analysis of the framing of encounters and can be taken up by Giddens into his idea of practical consciousness, and this in turn fits into an analysis of social reproduction of wider social systems through different types of encounter. What this means, however, is that the socialised aspect of the psyche goes right to the core, it is *the* central part; it is not surprising that Giddens has to restrict Freud's concept of the unconscious to a minimal role.

Giddens also loses what for me is one of the most important things about Goffman's work – that despite the frequent lack of

critical insight, he manages to capture in very precise ways the
means by which we maintain ourselves in interaction, the taken-
for-granted ways in which we *act*; one of the pleasures of reading
his work is a little thrill of excitement as he notes a tactic I realise
I frequently use to convey an impression, to keep another person
at bay. When, for instance, I casually mention to my students
something about my child, or about my family background, I
know, more or less explicitly, that I am doing what in some
circumstances might be called ingratiating myself, trying to
establish a humanity that might ward off anger felt about my
authority. Goffman calls it an expression of role-distance; before
reading him, I was not aware of exactly how I was doing it, but I
was aware, half-consciously, of the pressure of fear and the need
to do something to relieve it. Seeing the description of the tactic
makes it clearer to me what I am doing, although Goffman does
not see it in the same terms that I do; for Goffman, basically, it is
something which, in the end, helps the interaction to go more
smoothly. Goffman, of course, is right, but so am I. The
difficulty, perhaps, arises when someone does not want the
interaction to go more smoothly.

I think this becomes plainer when we look at Giddens's
interpretation of what he thinks Goffman is really talking about.
Far from being amoral, concerned with appearances, Giddens
argues, Goffman's writings:

> describe a highly moralised world of social relationships, but
> tend strongly to generalise its moral nature also. Trust and
> tact are more fundamental and binding features of social
> interaction than is the cynical manipulation of appearances.
> Thus people routinely shore up or 'repair' the moral fabric of
> interaction by displaying tact in what they say or do, by
> engaging in 'remedial practices' and helping others to save
> face.
>
> (Giddens 1987a: 113)

To a degree this is a good description of much day-to-day
interaction, those situations where we want things to go
smoothly, but if you can imagine a world where people only
wanted things to go smoothly, then it is easy to see the fallacy.
Who bears easily the burden of being tactful all the time?
Goffman is much more aware of this than is Giddens, and
particularly when he writes about back-stage settings: they

emerge as places where tact can be dropped, where the waiter can spit in the soup of an unpleasant customer, where I can curse my students, and so on. This also contributes to the smooth running of parts of the world, but it is a rather different world to the one Giddens describes, which perhaps might be the world of a Victorian aunt. The aim is to keep the interaction going, but it is not moralised – I don't curse my students to their faces because I might lose my job, or they might hit me, not because I want to keep the seminar working smoothly. What I want to do is kick over the tables and throw the stupid buggers through the window. It seems wrong to use the word 'moral' in this connection, and it seems to me that it is appropriate to use it only in an attenuated way in connection to routine. We maintain and repair the fabric of interaction because it helps us to achieve our ends more easily, and morality only enters when we feel that our ends are frustrated; on the other hand, questions of morality can perhaps be ever-present and much more relevant to our actions when they are not routine. The simple way of putting this is that I think the term *morality* is being devalued in this use. Beyond this, I am suggesting that Giddens is making a mistaken assumption similar to that of Parsons: that it is a commitment to a set of values, or in Giddens's case a more generalised moral commitment to not losing face, that maintains social order. Fear of punishment and instrumental self-interest are much more important.

There is a similar devaluation of the concept of trust. There is a sense in which we trust people, more or less, in routine activities: the man walking towards me will not attack me, the waiter will not slip poison in my drink, the insurance company will pay up, and so on. But trust is a much bigger word than this, associated with love, commitment, and all sorts of other things. It might be that our emotional vocabulary is limited or too vague, but I would prefer to distinguish these uses: trust 1 for the former and trust 2 for the latter. Intuitively, it makes sense to say that the trust I have or do not have in my insurance company is not the same thing as the trust I have or do not have in my wife, or my friends, or my ability to do things, or the trust I had or did not have in my mother. Giddens traces trust 1 from trust 2, but it seems to me that the two can exist separately and without connection. Trust 2 must be there to some degree for a child to develop at all, but it is possible for it to exist to a very tenuous degree, yet be accompanied by trust 1 of a normal level. The successful and intelligent 'borderline' or narcissistic patient seems to me a good example: the achievement of worldly success requires a fair amount of trust 1, and the qualities of such a personality include the charm and tact that make things run smoothly (and bring a deal of admiration), yet there is a fundamental failure of trust in personal relationships and an inner emptiness. Equally, it seems possible for trust 2 to develop without trust 1: the loving old couple who keep all their money in the mattress, perhaps.

This is looking forward to the next section. My main point here is that the world portrayed in Giddens's interpretation of Goffman seems to me an emotionally impoverished world in which terms such as morality and trust lose much of their strength and a comparatively empty notion of tact takes over: has Giddens never noticed the half-hidden looks of glee and the voyeuristic interest when tact is not maintained and face is lost? Highly popular television shows are devoted to it.

THE PERSONALITY

I want to spend some time now looking at what I regard as Giddens's misuse or misinterpretation of psychoanalysis, and from that to build up a rather different model of the personality to his own, which, it will be remembered, sees the person in terms of an unconscious, a practical consciousness and a reflexive consciousness. I have already suggested that, in several respects, his use of Freud's ideas loses the complexity of the original, and that that complexity is important. Here, I will start with another of his discussions of Freud, in *The Constitution of Society* (1984), this time of the Freudian model of id, ego and super-ego:

> Freud . . . regarded the individual as an agent but also often spoke of the id, ego and super-ego as agencies within the individual. In his writings prior to the 1920s, Freud frequently used the term *Das Ich* to refer to the whole person, as well as to designate a part of the mind. These shifts of usage also apply to the 'super-ego', sometimes differentiated from another notion, that of 'ego-ideal'. Terminological inconsistencies and transitions seem to indicate here some rather more significant conceptual troubles. . . . Suppose *Das Ich* is a subdivision of

mind. How can Freud then say such things as that the ego 'decides on the repudiation of the incompatible idea'? Is the ego's deciding some sort of process in miniature of the agent's deciding? This, sure, does not make much sense. Freud also writes, for example, of the ego's 'wish to sleep', although while sleep occurs it 'stays on duty' to protect against the worst emanations of the unconscious, 'guarding' the sleep of the dreamer. The same sort of questions arise. Whose sleep is it that the ego desires? The agent's? Its own? Whose waking does the 'guard' protect? And so on. Consider, finally, Freud's most general characterisation of the tasks of the ego. The ego has the task of 'self-preservation', which it executes 'by learning to bring about changes in the external world to its own advantage'. But which 'self' does the ego defend? Is its advantage also my advantage?

(Giddens 1984: 42)

I have quoted this at length because I think it is a good example of the form of theorising that Giddens often adopts, and because it indicates the sort of complexity that he does not like and I think of as essential, at least in this area. The form of theorising is one that aims at conceptual clarity and regards the identification of contradictions as itself a reason for rejecting another theory. It seems to me that the lack of conceptual clarity and the contradictions that Giddens picks out in Freud are both necessary and productive.

They are necessary on two levels. The first is that they are phenomenologically appropriate – they describe a real experience that people have of themselves. Deciding is not a simple matter and is often surrounded by internal conflicts, and it is quite conceivable that we might feel that one part of ourselves has decided something and that another part is fighting against it, or even that a number of different parts are fighting on the side of different decisions. I have heard it described as having a committee meeting going on in one's head. We can become aware of having decided something without being conscious of taking the decision, of having forgotten something, perhaps conveniently, without being aware of doing the forgetting. It makes sense experientially to talk of the self not as a simple unity but as a complexity of desires, ideas and so on. We all perhaps have the experience of doing something to preserve ourselves, and to point out that we can ask who is doing the preserving and who is being preserved does not mean that we do not have the experience.

Freud of course is doing more than trying to arrive at a good phenomenological description. The second level on which the lack of clarity and the contradictions are necessary is theoretical – the understanding of our experience. They are necessary *because* the experience itself is contradictory, not only from the inside, but from the outside: we can see other people divided against themselves, watch their erratic or contradictory behaviour. It is difficult to see how such behaviour can be understood by a set of unitary concepts with simple, linear relations to each other. We find Giddens criticising a similar ambiguity in Erikson, which, earlier, I also argued was a necessary ambiguity. Indeed, it has become apparent from developments in psychoanalysis since Freud that the id, ego and super-ego model is in fact too crude; we can arrive at even more complex and contradictory models using conceptions of internal objects and part-objects and concepts of introjection and projection. These sorts of contradictions are necessary if we are to have any useful notion of the unconscious, which Giddens wants, since it means there is a part of the self which does things which the self doesn't know it is doing.

The use of contradictory or ambiguous concepts enables the understanding of a depth of experience that Giddens's combination of discursive consciousness, practical consciousness and the unconscious cannot. I want to try to show this by looking at Giddens's comments on mental illness, which he takes from Goffman, and at a more complex psychoanalytic account. For Giddens, mental illness is seen largely in terms of a breakdown in the rules of practical consciousness, the most fundamental rules of interaction (Thomas Scheff (1966) refers to them as 'residual rules'). 'Psychotic disturbance' is seen as a failure of the minute ways in which we monitor our bodily movements, our appearance, the opening and closing of our encounters with others – the psychotic individual can be seen as experimenting with and on these very fundamental rules (see Giddens 1984: 79–81). Later on, he suggests that:

It may very well be that the clues to the character of madness, or, in its modern guise, 'mental illness', are to be found not in the extravagance of delusions, visions of other worlds, but in much more mundane features of bodily and gestural impropriety. Social disability, not a mysterious access to a lost continent of unreason, may express its real nature.

(Giddens 1984: 158)

I want now to compare with this a clinical example taken from work with a psychotic patient by the psychoanalyst W. R. Bion (1959). He describes a particular incident in a session in the following way:

> I had reason to give the patient an interpretation making explicit his feelings of affection and his expression of them to his mother for her ability to cope with a refractory child. The patient attempted to express his agreement with me, but although he needed to say only a few words his expression of them was interrupted by a very pronounced stammer which had the effect of spreading out his remark over a period of as much as a minute and a half. The actual sounds emitted bore resemblance to gasping for breath; gaspings were interspersed with gurgling sounds as if he were immersed in water. I drew his attention to these sounds and he agreed that they were peculiar and himself suggested the description I have just given.

(Bion 1959: 309)

Bion's elaboration of this incident involves the concept of projective identification: the need in the infant to eject feelings that he or she finds (literally) unbearable (Bion thinks that for the patient in this example it was the fear of death) into another person (the mother or primary caretaker) where the feeling can be born and modified in a way that makes it safe for the infant to re-introject the feeling as part of him- or herself. He argues that a certain degree of projective identification is necessary and essential for development. (Winnicott (1964), I think, uses basically the same notion in his concept of 'holding', to which I will refer below). Bion suggests that this particular patient was not 'allowed' an adequate degree of projective identification, perhaps by a mother who responded to her baby's distress but without being able, herself, to bear it. In turn, the patient felt that Bion was rejecting his identifications; the stammer indicates this to Bion, and he sees it as an attack on the words which would link the two together, a response to what the patient experiences as a rejection of projective identification.

I want now to try to compare these two accounts. On one level, there is nothing incompatible about them. It is certainly true that the patient was breaking the rules of routine interaction, even of something as fundamental as being able to make a verbal response to another person; he had somehow lost those rules, temporarily. It is also true that he was experimenting with the relationship, but not with the rules themselves – they were a means to an end in the relationship, and it is true that he was suffering from a social disability, although my reaction to naming it thus is that this must have been the least of his problems. What you don't have in Giddens's description is the sense and understanding of the intrapersonal difficulties of the man and the dynamic of his relationship with Bion. Giddens's way of looking at mental illness rests on the surface and defines it in terms of its relation to the socially expected or required – in terms of conventional sociology, including the conventional sociology of mental illness, in relation to role behaviour. Bion's account is of the mechanisms 'under' that description. Giddens's own account, it seems to me, only becomes 'wrong' when it claims to be an explanation, or more than a partial description of what is happening in mental illness. Unfortunately, it does make that claim insofar as it is built into a theory which excludes Bion's type of analysis.

I want now to turn directly to Giddens's notion of routine and ontological security, his use of R. D. Laing (1960) and object-relations theory. My point in arguing that Giddens does not understand these writers is to suggest not only that there is much more to the personality than is embraced in his theory but also that the notions of ontological security and routine are not sufficient to carry the theoretical weight that he places upon them. There are intuitive reasons for accepting what he says about the importance of routine, and intuitive reasons for rejecting it. Routine is clearly important to a sense of safety and reliability; if every activity were always a matter of spontaneous impulse or random choice then life would quickly become unbearable. On the other hand, people might develop a routine of washing their hands sixty-five times a day, counting every crack in the pavement as they walk, or having fried eggs and bacon for breakfast at 8.05 a.m. and falling into an uncontrollable rage if it does not appear. More routinely, routine is experienced as enveloping, as creating a sense of claustrophobia, and a person's emotional dependence on routine is frequently experienced by others as a sign that he or she is not well or is inadequate, or at any rate as an indicator of something being wrong. Routine, in our world, is not a simple thing.

The same sort of intuitive ambivalence exists around ontological security. Giddens writes as if it is, or can be, simply 'there'. Today I feel ontologically secure; next year when I lose my job (or whatever) I will not. We must all see the sense in this. On the other hand, Giddens's own discussion of what he calls the existential contradiction implies that ontological security always involves some degree of ambivalence; it is always a matter of feeling more or less secure. And whilst we might look to routine to seek reassurance, it is precisely the routine nature of our lives that can throw our sense of ontological security into confusion. *Ontological security is not the same thing as feeling safe.* Willmott (1986) has pointed this out in connection with R. D. Laing's work, from which Giddens first lifts the idea of ontological security. Immersion in routine actually invites the *recurrence* of anxiety, and reliance on routine is a defence against, not a cure for, anxiety. In Laing's work, and generally in psychoanalysis, ontological security involves the ability to deal with change and to recognise the routine as both necessary and comparatively ephemeral, exactly the opposite of Giddens's propositions.

Object-relations theory, in the work of Winnicott (1964) and others, demonstrates much more clearly than Laing the psychic mechanisms and processes by means of which this ontological security is achieved. As in my earlier example from Bion, the infant – all infants – are racked by anxieties they cannot bear, their 'self' is too weak, too underdeveloped to manage. The 'holding' work of the parent is not to somehow get rid of the painful feelings (perhaps the most immediate reaction of most of us when faced with a distressed baby) but to take and hold the feelings, to tolerate and bear them for the infant so that they can be re-internalised as bearable, manageable feelings. This depends on, amongst other things, more or less consistent and routine caring behaviour by the parent, but above all on the emotional interchange between parent and child. Caring can be consistent and routine and destructive; the child-rearing methods of Truby King – four-hourly feeding, limited expression of affection, etc. –

were certainly routine and consistent, and might, if one is lucky, provide a good formula for raising a guard dog from a puppy. And it is less often the experience of anxiety which brings people to psychotherapy than the inability to contain that experience, and perhaps in some cases the inability to experience anxiety at all, being overwhelmed instead with psychosomatic symptoms, insomnia, or whatever.

When, in *The Consequences of Modernity* (1990), Giddens draws on Winnicott, none of this comes across at all. Instead of the object-relations 'goal' of a mature individual who can allow him- or herself to experience and use anxiety and ontological security, we find individuals who receive 'an emotional inoculation which protects against . . . ontological anxieties' (Giddens 1990: 94), and independence or autonomy becomes a behavioural result of routine care as a child. The growth of integration and the mechanisms by which we live in the world disappear in Giddens's account.

It may be, of course, that psychoanalysis is not necessary to Giddens's theory of the agent, of the personality. If it is not, we are left with a very shallow picture of the human being indeed – the product of routine practices who only feels safe in routine practices. If it is necessary, then his misunderstandings of psychoanalysis leave it in pieces. This has consequences for all his theory insofar as the rest of it depends upon the notion of ontological security and routine. In fact I don't think it does, except maybe in one or two formulations, and his comments about social systems, structures, etc. do not lose what value they have. When, however, structuration theory takes on the pretences of a systematic theory à la Parsons, these ideas become essential building bricks in the system, and the whole system is undermined.

It is particularly Giddens's rather fundamentally oversim-plified notion of the individual that takes me on to my final chapter. This argument has, I think, considerable consequences for his analysis of modernity and for the status of structuration theory in relation to modernity and his ability to develop any really critical dimensions in his writing.

Chapter 9

The problem with modernity

I want now to continue my critique of Giddens on a different level and in a different way. The thrust of my argument so far has been that the synthesis he offers ejects ideas that are important for sociology, and that by itself, structuration theory does not embrace social reality in the way that he claims. This is not to say that it is simply wrong and to send it back with a red cross beside it; all the elements have something to aid our understanding, but they do not fit together in the way that he claims, and the understanding that it offers is partial. The social world is more complex and varied than is imagined in the theory; we require a range of theories that might be quite incompatible to begin to make sense of it.

In this chapter, I want to go back to the idea of a synthesising project as a whole and to the elements that have been left out of the synthesis, and look at them in the context of the nature of the modern world and in terms of possible reactions to modernity. I want to argue that many aspects of structuration theory are symptomatic of the damaging or dangerous aspects of modernity and that this prevents Giddens from getting any truly critical grip on the modern world. In this, I will have recourse to the elements of psychoanalytic theory that he misinterprets or glosses over, in particular the work that has appeared over the last fifteen years on narcissism as a feature of the personality and as a cultural feature.

I should make it clear that I do not want to put forward a rigorous theory of modernity as an alternative to Giddens; rather I want to suggest that some modern trends in psychoanalytic cultural criticism offer a better grasp on some aspects of modernity than does Giddens's approach, that it offers a clearer basis for a critical approach to modernity, and that it enables us to understand some aspects of structuration theory as symptomatic of aspects of modernity.

THE EXPERIENCE OF MODERNITY

Giddens's account of modernity starts with his sociological analysis. The development of abstract systems, the process of globalisation and the inherent process of reflexive monitoring which seems to bring everything into question: these developments and more contribute to our everyday experience, which includes our perception of modernity as a juggernaut, our constant reflection on our relationships and the difficulties we have with intimacy, our opportunities and desire for self-fulfilment. I want to try to push the analysis of this experience a little further, taking ideas from psychoanalysis, although it seems clear to me that the evidence for the existence of these experiences can be drawn from many sources, including the ideas discussed in this book.

The first experience is that of fragmentation, an internal fragmentation. Throughout psychoanalysis, but especially in the work of Melanie Klein, we can find reference to the tendency to split and fragment the world or ourselves. An early way of dealing with our good and bad experiences is through such splitting, seeing the bad in the world outside us, threatening us, and feeling that the good is inside us, there to be protected. If the threat becomes too great, then we might protect ourselves by trying to fragment the good – the very frightening feeling of 'falling apart' – and although it sounds odd to talk of such a feeling as a defence, it can be understood, rather like some suicides, as a last-ditch attempt to save what is good in us.

Now it seems to me the experience of the world 'out there' as a thoroughly bad place, and the experience of internal fragmentation, have become major common experiences, at least for those of us who live at the heart of modernity. We can see it reflected in Giddens's own account of modernity: in the perception of modernity as a juggernaut, even though, he argues, it is not, and in the unthinkable fears of nuclear war, ecological and economic disaster and political tyranny, which he sees as the central dangers of modernity. All these fears involve an accurate perception of reality – the dangers he names are out there in the world – but they can also become caught up in our unconscious phantasies so our perceptions of them become distorted and what we do about the fears loses touch with reality. This is especially so when they become caught up in the fear of internal fragmentation – the disaster of modernity about which Giddens has nothing to say.

One expression of this experience of fragmentation is to be found clearly in modernist and post-modernist art and literature, and in the increasingly narrow range in which we seek to find a coherent meaning for our lives. It is given explicit and very coherent formulation in the work of the structuralist and post-structuralist philosophers, as I pointed out earlier, precisely in their ideas that Giddens rejects. The phrases about 'the death of the subject', the 'decentred subject', the 'constitution of the subject' all reflect this. Christopher Lasch (1984) discusses the way we limit ourselves and our ambitions because of our awareness of the real dangers of modernity but also to avoid the experience of inner collapse, of falling apart.

A second aspect of our experience of modernity is our impotence. One of the intriguing things about the way in which Giddens's work has developed is that *The Consequences of Modernity* (1990) recognises the truth of that experience, yet there is nothing in structuration theory which leads us to expect this, and its earliest presentations emphasised its humanistic impetus, the fact that human beings create and sustain institutions and social systems. It seems that increasingly he has come to realise that systems are maintained because so often there seems, and perhaps really is, no alternative. This experience, and this reality, is also reflected theoretically, if one-sidedly, in the more determinist structural sociologies.

A third aspect involves a collection of reactions which I want to place under the heading of omnipotence, the precise opposite of impotence. The psychoanalytic literature on narcissism is saturated with accounts of radical mood swings, from grandiose feelings of power and triumph and goodness to feelings of empty desolation; this cycle can be seen as part of our experience of modernity. By omnipotence here I refer to a wide range of cultural phenomena documented by Lasch (1980 and 1984). The psychodynamics of the process involve a reaction to or a defence against the feeling of impotence, by seeking areas of activity in which one can imagine one has complete power or can achieve complete satisfaction. This can manifest itself in a range of activities, from consistent and dedicated concern about health and fitness to a feeling that one has a right to have one's needs met and to achieve an unadulterated happiness in relationships with others. It is very much a part of what Giddens seems to be talking about when he sees self-fulfilment as an important possibility opened up by modernity. I want to look more closely at this idea later. It is implicit in much radical and sexual politics and in a range of phenomena from the blossoming of psychotherapies and counselling to the availability and use of credit facilities that take the waiting out of wanting.

The social roots of these experiences are not necessarily those that would be emphasised by Giddens. The rapid development of technology, bureaucratisation and the increasingly limited role of the family are emphasised by Lasch. The dominant character structure of modernity is seen as one which is in crucial ways 'empty', containing only the idealised good and punitive parental figures of infancy. We have great difficulty in seeing the world in terms of shades of grey, of pain as well as pleasure, in accepting the normal inadequacies of the human being in a difficult and unsatisfactory world. Emotional learning, particularly through processes of grief and mourning, becomes difficult, since any loss is experienced as abandonment and the infantile rage and fear that it produces cannot be tolerated. It becomes difficult to carry good experiences forward and use them as a basis during future difficult times, to learn from life.

In such a state, we can seek constant new satisfactions which we imagine will fill up the space inside us, looking for 'highs' which will hide the internal emptiness. The ego does not develop a strong rational and moral dimension that enables us to make sacrifices for the sake of others and to make judgements on our own account even if it incurs the disapproval of others.

STRUCTURATION THEORY AS A 'SYMPTOM' OF MODERNITY

I have argued elsewhere (Craib 1987) that ways of theorising, as well as the content of theory, can be seen, *in addition to* their real value as a contribution to knowledge, as psychodynamic processes. By this I mean ways of dealing with the world that find their parallel in the ways individuals deal with the world on a more personal level: we can find similar processes and defences at work in theory as we can find in the everyday activities of people in the world.

I indicated in the introduction the lines that my critique was going to take, and in many ways what I am going to say applies to sociology as a whole as much as to Giddens in particular, since there is much in the discipline that reacts defensively to the world it studies. The most striking feature of the social world is its complexity and variability, and for sociology, as perhaps for any of the social sciences, the scandal of that complexity and variability is that we cannot know everything. Each of the social sciences has perhaps to be content with its own object, learning what it can from the others. Structuration theory seems to me to deny this complexity in a variety of ways which I have tried to document through these final, critical chapters. It does so firstly through trying to rule out theories and approaches which, I have argued, for all their defects, still have some contact with social reality and provide a useful way of looking at it. The very idea of synthesis, of pulling together a whole a range of different ideas and theories, again seems a denial of complexity; I have tried to show this by demonstrating what Giddens leaves out of the theories he incorporates. Beyond this, there is his argument that the boundaries with the other social sciences – history, geography, etc. – are blurring and that they are beginning to come together, hence the designation of his work as social rather than sociological theory. The division of labour between the social sciences and, come to that, between the social and the natural sciences, might have irrational elements, but there are rational elements as well: it enables an allocation of energy and interest to a range of phenomena that could not conceivably be embraced by any one individual or group of individuals. It would clearly be nonsense to suggest that Giddens wants to merge everything, but there is an element of grandiosity about all this.

There is also an element of omnipotence in the insistence, at least in theoretical terms if not in his historical sociology, of the importance of praxis, of human action, human meaning over and against structural constraint. It is not that the theory dreams an imaginary power for human beings, one that we do not have; we have the powers that Giddens suggests, but there are other, and often stronger, powers in the social world. A stylistic sign that these issues are being glossed over lies, I think, in his increasing tendency towards assertion rather than argument in his work. I can understand this tendency; in many ways it shows more self-respect than persistent defensive debate, in which he could easily find himself embroiled if he felt that he had to reply in detail to every critical contribution. There comes a point where one must simply get on with it, in spite of the complexities. But there is a difference between allowing the complexities to exist and getting on with it by working with them, and implicitly or explicitly denying them by assuming, for example, that such intriguing and productive schools as structuralism and post-structuralism are dead.

There is perhaps a gentle swing from omnipotence to impotence as his theory progresses, concentrating more on time-space and system organisation, and in the development of his historical sociology and his account of modernity. Human action, praxis, remains at the basis of everything throughout, 'in theory' as it were, but increasingly he portrays human existence as struggling against social forces more powerful than itself, a point made by Perry Anderson (1990). The swing is not as dramatic as one can sometimes find in Parsons' theory, from a voluntarism to a determinism, but in practice Giddens's voluntarism has had to come to some compromise with reality even if theoretically it has avoided it. It is clearly Giddens's radical voluntarism that inspires those most impressed by and ready to take up his theory. His voluntarism seems to me a reaction to the modern world not dissimilar to that of post-structuralism, and inherent in the linguistic turn of modern philosophy as a whole. As human freedom has become more limited and as it has become more difficult to think in terms of radical social transformation in the modern West, so attention has concentrated on more narrow aspects of life, such as language, where a complete (and I think imaginary) freedom is posited: the world is as it is because it is a product of our language, our discourse. For Giddens, it is a product of our practices; he has not moved along the line as far as post-structuralism but is on the same end of the continuum. In psychoanalytic terms this might be termed a sort of cultural reaction formation: the less power we seem to have over the society we live in, the more we assert our freedom in theory.

In his emphasis on the distinctiveness of modernity, I think there is, as I indicated above, a resort to history in order to deny its importance. In the new world of modernity, it seems difficult to learn from history. There is, as Saunders (in Held and Thompson 1989) points out, a tendency to contrast modern and pre-modern societies with an implicit romanticisation of the latter, but apart from that we can, it seems, take nothing from those societies to understand our own. I would not, for one minute, suggest that the distinctive features of modernity that Giddens lists are not new, but to emphasise them in the way that he does serves to mask the continuities of problems and solutions that can also be identified. It hides our roots in the past, emphasises our freedom at the expense of our origins, in the same way that some people deny their childhood.

David Gross (1982) is particularly suggestive on this issue. He argues that modern sociology has not ignored issues of time-space but rather only issues of temporality. Spatial analysis and metaphors abound throughout sociology and social theory, and as I suggested above, following McLennan (Clark *et al.* 1990), Giddens's analysis of time in practice employs spatial metaphors, despite his theoretical objections to this. As I understand Gross's argument, and putting my own gloss on it, modern culture has lost its sense of history, of being rooted in the past, and our knowledge of the past comes increasingly only through official re-interpretations of history. In Gross's terms, history is being appropriated by the state, which I think makes it too simple, and perhaps too conspiratorial. Nevertheless, individuals are left with their own personal and biological histories and no reliable long-term perspective in which to place them. In fact, Giddens's account of modern history seems to me to support Gross's case and provide an illustration of what Gross is criticising at the same time. Giddens shows the way in which modernity breaks from the past and the effect of the continuous process of rationalisation in challenging and undermining tradition, in effect challenging and undermining history. But this is shown, apart from the more idealised references to the past, uncritically, and in fact it is emphasised. He falls for the modern world's trick of hiding and rewriting its own roots and contributes to it.

There is one further way in which I think Giddens's theory reflects modernity rather than grasps it, and that has haunted me throughout the writing of this book. This is the fragmentation of concepts, the 'throwing of concepts at a problem', as Bernstein puts it. It does not approach some forms of post-modernism, where concepts seem to emerge immediately to disappear again, and there is a systematic centre to structuration theory, but it is surrounded by a range of *ad hoc* concepts designed to fill in gaps, to give an impression of totality, whilst at the same time avoiding it. The fragmentation is most apparent in his style: the comparatively short span of attention for any one argument or topic, the rapid movement from thinker to thinker, topic to topic, the absence of what Hegel called 'the labour of the negative', the logical following through and questioning of arguments. The world of theory begins, at times, to seem like a collection of bits.

To repeat myself, I am not trying to put forward a more or less rigorous alternative to Giddens; rather it is a matter of using some ideas from psychoanalytic cultural analysis, perhaps in a metaphorical way, to highlight points about structuration theory that I have tried to make elsewhere in a more systematic theoretical way. My point is that in certain aspects of his work, Giddens has been caught up in what one might call the 'ideology' of modernity, and in others he is presenting in theoretical form some of the defences that we use in our personal lives to avoid the more painful realities of the world. A final aspect in which I think this happens is in his difficulty in developing a critical theory, in developing an ethical stance towards the world.

CRITICAL THEORY

Jeff Livesay (1985), in a comparison of Giddens and Habermas, suggests that there might be a contradiction between concentrating on the openness of praxis and developing a normative grounding for a critical theory. We can, then, find Giddens on the former and Habermas on the latter horn of this dilemma. I think the point is well made, if we assume that the aim of theory is to reconcile all types of desirable ideas, but what interests me is that there does not seem to be a dilemma if we recognise properly that we are dealing with relativities. In Giddens's case, his insistence on the openness of praxis and of history, as we have seen, does inhibit the development of a critical theory that draws on some conception of human nature and of what human society should be like. The over-assertion of human freedom leads to the failure to establish or found a moral critique, and both of these reflect the impetus of modernity.

When I say that Giddens avoids an ethical stance towards the world, this is not quite true. He clearly does possess an ethical stance and a political stance, both of which seem to be identifiable as 'left of centre' and with which I find myself in some agreement. Yet he declines – it seems on grounds of principle, although it might be more a matter of economy of energy – to try to ground his critical approach on anything more than his analysis of what is happening in the world. Given the more abstract, ontological concerns of structuration theory, it does not seem to produce the more detailed analyses of current situations that can give his critical stance more bite. In the same way, it does not point directly to issues for empirical research – I'm inclined to agree with Giddens's more agnostic attitude towards the relationship between his theory and empirical research, but not the agnosticism implied in his attitude towards critical theory.

In *The Consequences of Modernity* (1990), his critical approach seems to me to be developed on a common-sense level that does not owe much to structuration theory; in fact, I would argue that where it does owe something to structuration theory, the critical impetus fails. The disasters that he discusses – economic and ecological collapse, political tyranny, nuclear war – are not the discovery of structuration theory, nor are the movements that oppose them, and the discussion he undertakes, whatever its merits, is not outside what one might expect of a reasonably well-informed journalist or layperson. I find his projections rather utopian, and he himself seems to acknowledge that the 'immanent trends' that he discusses are no more than that (Giddens 1990: 171). I like his idea of 'utopian realism' and agree that it is important that we keep both sides of the continuum in sight, but the crucial question is: from where do the utopian ideals come? For Giddens it seems largely a matter of looking at the nasty things that are happening in the world and imagining the nice things that might stop them – presumably this is a use of counterfactual questioning. I don't think this is a bad thing, but it is a rather small baby for such an elephant as structuration theory.

I find it difficult to think through structuration theory in such a way as to produce a critical dimension, and I suspect this might be not because it can't be done but because the critical dimension might be so clearly utopian, as opposed to realist, that it would not prove much help. When he comments that a philosophical anthropology might be necessary to understand the nature of human needs, Giddens manages to overlook the fact that he offers us one, albeit unclearly, in structuration theory. A philosophical anthropology and an ontology of social being are closely connected. Marx's philosophical anthropology, as implied or contained in the *1844 Manuscripts* for example, involves an ontology of social being, placing labour and sociality at the centre of human life. One might be able to regard Giddens's emphasis on praxis in the same light, arguing that the ideal society is one where the transformative freedom of human action is realised to its fullest extent, but, given his emphasis on practical and discursive consciousness, this freedom is difficult to envisage. The rules that he talks about are rules necessary for any human social organisation to exist, and it does not seem to make much sense to talk of a situation in which people would be aware of and able to change such basic features of life. We could perhaps posit an ideal world where everything has entered into discursive consciousness, but that would run counter to some of Giddens's own ideals for society, since one of the problems he wishes to deal with is rampant reflexivity and questioning. His theory recognises, rightly I think, that power is inherent in human relationships, but there is no reason, within his ontology, to suggest that we might desire to minimise power relationships or work towards a different degree of equality. Those ideas come from his own, unexplicated value judgements.

The result of this, I think, is that Giddens becomes trapped in the surface appearances of modernity. I have argued at length that his conception of the agent is a shallow one, and pervaded by the social - that perhaps like Parsons' conception, it is over-socialised. The conception of the person in modern systems is of someone who is both defined and constituted by and dealing with the problems of living with abstract systems. I think Giddens is right to emphasise the double-sided nature of modernity: there is a sense in which the modern world presents us with many more materials and space for ourselves than any form of traditional society, but I have tried to argue that it is also the case that there are aspects of modernity which make the use of these opportunities difficult, if not impossible. Giddens cannot locate these difficulties except in the general tendencies of our society, the grand institutional clusters. He is simply naïve about the relationship between these and the individual. He takes a quote from Christopher Lasch's *Haven in a Heartless World* (1977), and his comments on it provide the crux of my argument; I am reproducing both in full. The quote from Lasch runs as follows:

> As the world takes on a more and more menacing appearance, life becomes a never-ending search for health and well-being through exercise, dieting, drugs, spiritual regimens of various kinds, psychic self-help and psychiatry. From those who have withdrawn interest from the outside world except insofar as it remains a source of gratification and frustration, the state of their own health becomes an all absorbing concern.
>
> (Lasch 1977: 140)

Giddens comments:

> Is the search for self-identity a form of somewhat pathetic narcissism, or is it, in some part at least, a subversive force in respect of modern institutions? . . . [T]here is something awry in Lasch's statement. A 'search for health and well-being' hardly sounds compatible with a 'withdrawal of interest in the outside world'. The benefits of exercise or dieting are not personal discoveries but come from the lay reception of expert knowledge, as does the appeal of therapy or psychiatry. The spiritual regimens in question may be an eclectic assemblage, but include religions and cults from around the world. The outside world not only enters in here; it is an outside world vastly more extensive in character than anyone would have had contact with in the pre-modern era.
>
> (Giddens 1990: 123)

Giddens's last statement is true; it emphasises the possibility of taking up the new materials and integrating them into an authentic form of life. Lasch's argument, however, is that what comes from the outside world, including expert knowledge, is being used not to change the world but to protect oneself, unrealistically, from unpleasantness and eventually from death. We're not finding better, wider identities but rather manic false selves. Lasch is not talking about withdrawal from the outside world (except when it gets in the way and what it offers cannot be used self-servingly) but of the selective choice of features from the world in order to hide its full reality. The expert knowledge itself conspires in this, appearing to offer an insurance against growing old, growing ill, growing to a socially disapproved size. One of the most difficult lessons of psychoanalytic therapy is that the easy answers, the avoidance of bad feelings, the avoidance of the responsibility for one's own feelings that are offered by the various 'spiritual regimens', are fantasies; that loss, grief, illness, death, envy, greed, jealousy and frustration are essential parts of the human condition.

The search for personal identity in this context takes on a different meaning. It becomes a search which destroys both the fabric of our interdependence, as relationships cannot be sustained, and which leaves the outside world moving along whatever course it is following. A sense of identity does not come from more choice, from trying to have as much as possible, whether we are talking about material or spiritual possessions, but from finding one's limits, one's boundaries, and one's necessary dependence on others with all the vulnerabilities it brings.

Doubtless this argument could go on forever; my central point is that structuration theory could not even conceive of the possibility of Lasch's critique since structuration theory's conception of the agent is too simple and too sociologistic and its grasp of the relationship between agent and structure does not allow the complexities of our relationships to the outside world; nor can it allow for the founding of the sort of moral critique offered by Lasch, since that would involve acknowledging too great a range of restrictions on praxis.

Just as modernity is double-edged, however, so is structuration theory. The last three chapters have been more or less systematically critical, and my tone often hostile. It is true that I do not think the theory delivers on what it promises; Christopher Bryant has suggested that in fact I am arguing that the difficulty with Giddens is that he is embarking on a modernist synthesising and totalising project that we are perceiving through post-modernist eyes which can no longer even imagine such a project. There is, I think, a degree of truth in this, and very few people have been able to take on the project as a whole, from either a critical or supportive position. As I pointed out in the introduction, the critical literature consists largely of attempts to take one aspect of

Giddens's work and investigate it in detail. It is as if the whole is too much to handle. Paradoxically it seems to me that it is in fact this modernism that is also the source of what is good about structuration theory: at the same time as we cannot hope to grasp the whole in one theory, it is important that such an attempt be made, the whole be kept in view. It is this side of the project that will concern me in the last chapter.

Chapter 10

The importance of
structuration theory

The last four chapters have been very critical, and I now want to change direction. It would be quite in order to ask why, given what I have had to say, is it worth spending the time and energy to find out anything about structuration theory? Why, in fact, is Giddens worth reading? There are a number of very positive answers to this question, and the first one is that it is difficult now to think of social theory, or sociology itself, without Giddens. There is a sense in which his work provides a centre for the discipline. And, for all the criticisms I have made of the project of synthesis, it is none the less an important, essential project.

If I ask myself what I have learnt from reading and re-reading Giddens, as opposed to what I disagree with, the answer is a range of ideas and arguments that are now a crucial part of modern sociology but were not so before his work appeared. I also have a different way of organising my thoughts about theory and about sociological investigation. These do not necessarily come from Giddens but are a response to his work, and it is difficult to think of anyone writing in the field of social theory or theoretical sociology who would not have to respond to his work in some way. Another way of making this point is that while working on the book, I have found myself constructing an imaginary degree course based on Giddens's work – not his recent mammoth textbook but on his development of structuration theory. The centre of the course would move from the foundations of the discipline through the crucial theoretical debates of this century, bringing in both methodology and philosophy of social science. Nearly all, and in some cases more than, the usual range of optional courses could be offered from certain points in his work, from the social structure of modern societies through to social psychology, via, amongst many others, the sociology of organisations, historical sociology, comparative social institutions, the sociology of war and the military, urban sociology, rural sociology, political sociology, industrial sociology – the list, while not infinite, is immense.

Such a degree course would be different from those on offer fifteen years ago. Close to the centre would be Marx's analysis of early capitalism and the work of Goffman and Garfinkel, and the insights of modern European philosophy; conceptions of time and space would be to the fore whenever the course moved from theory to any of the substantive areas of sociology. The theory of knowledge – epistemology – would play less of a role than it did, and there would be a much greater emphasis at the heart of sociology on what sort of society we might envisage for the future. These changes would not be there simply as the result of Giddens's work; he has moved with a tide, but it is difficult to see how they could be organised coherently without his work. Giddens, more than any other writer, has brought together the disparate range of ideas and approaches that was sociology in the early 1970s, and he offers the most inclusive core to the discipline currently available. If we look at the range of critical literature, it is becoming increasingly sophisticated, and however critical it might be, the deepening of ideas and arguments is there as a response to Giddens, and would not be there without his work.

This might sound like faint praise – however wrong he might be, at least he gives other people the chance of being right. I mean more than this, for all the criticisms I have produced in the previous chapters have a reverse side. In particular those features of structuration theory that I argued were symptomatic of the more dangerous and threatening features of modernity are also projects which need to be held onto if modernity is not to swamp us.

THE FLUX OF DEVELOPMENT

It is, perhaps, too easy to think of the creation of sociology as a coherent discipline as only an organisational or a cognitive matter. Of the two, the former is the least preferable, since it involves an intellectually arbitrary judgement on the part of departments, grant-awarding bodies and journals as to what is at the centre of the discipline and the exclusion of what does not fit. Such judgments do of course happen, and their occurrence is not arbitrary in the context of political power struggles, but luckily the discipline is sufficiently diffuse in organisational terms, and individual sociologists and departments are both too innovative and too ambitious, for the discipline to draw a boundary around itself. Political and power issues are instead constantly reflected in the theoretical and methodological debates, and Giddens recognises that this prohibits development of an inclusive paradigm in the discipline.

It is more tempting to see the problem as a cognitive one: we can trace such attempts from the original concern to establish sociology as a separate social science, through to Parsons' attempt to synthesise the various foundations, through to Giddens's own synthesis. The assumption is that the synthesis is 'right', whether or not this claim is based in an explicit set of epistemological criteria. It is, I suspect, the mark of the difficulty of syntheses that has led Giddens away from explicit concern with epistemology (a point made, critically, by Bryant 1990). The claim, however, must still be there and, of course, once it is questioned, the complex and apparently insoluble arguments that Giddens avoids all return. In fact, I think Giddens is offering an implicit pragmatic justification for structuration theory: if it works, for purposes of the organisation of knowledge, for providing guidelines for research and for organising and interpreting the results of research, then it is true. This, of course, raises the organisational issue: useful for whom and where?

There are, then, organisational and sociological preconditions for attempts at syntheses, and Richard Kilminster (in Bryant and Jary 1991) offers a hermeneutic critique of Giddens suggesting, rightly I think, that structuration theory cannot reflect back upon the sociological conditions for such a synthesis. Kilminster's argument is in the context of a wider argument about the necessity of a theory of cognitive change 'based in the competition between groups for the public interpretation of reality' (in Bryant and Jary 1991: 112). Borrowing from Mannheim, he suggests looking at the recent development of Western sociology in terms of the following stages:

(1) a monopoly stage, as an academic establishment secured its

position, structural-functionalism being the dominant interpretation;

(2) a competitive stage, in which groups challenged the dominant interpretation, the challenge based on generational, political and experiential changes; and

(3) a concentration stage, in which debates came together and focused on key antimonies: constructivism/realism; agency/ structure; meaning/cause; subjectivism/objectivism.

This last situation produces the conditions for a synthesis which, he suggests, is based on the nature of the social existence of all parties, although he does not go into what this might be. The point I want to make here is that this particular schema is quite reasonable and better than some in that it draws attention to the life of the community that produces these ideas. The difficulty with any such schema is that it is only part of the truth; things are never quite as clear as they seem. Thus the monopoly period was not *really* a monopoly: work in other traditions was going on at the same time, even though structural-functionalism might have been dominant. Kilminster suggests that the radical heirs to the 1960s grouped around the first categories in his antimonies, but in fact a very strong, radical Marxist tradition adopted the work of Althusser and grouped around the second categories.

There are several such models of the development of sociology, and there is often a general agreement amongst them – there is not much difference between Kilminster's and that offered by Giddens, for example – and they all have a degree of truth in them; yet they all never quite fit what is happening. There is always a degree of rhetoric in each: we all set up models of sociology in order to make our own points, even to make our own points sound more radical than perhaps they really are, just as we tend to set up straw targets, a crude Marx or a crude Parsons or even, perhaps, a crude Giddens. There is always some truth in these constructions, but there is always more going on. The simplest way of putting this is that there is always a process of coming together and always a process of fragmentation: the two processes go on simultaneously and, perhaps, for one period one process will be dominant, and in another period another, although which we see might depend on where we are standing and what we want to do.

The difficulty is trying to maintain a grasp on both processes at the same time, the work which, in our everyday lives, we often refer to as 'keeping our heads together'. There are moments of integration when we feel at least comparatively in charge of things, and moments when we feel pulled in different directions and out of control. However, I am not sure that either of these processes, of integration or disintegration, ever becomes a *state*, although we might deny or project or defend ourselves against the awareness of either process, perhaps most obviously the latter. If the term *balance* means anything, it is being aware to some degree of both processes. If we extend this idea to other areas of life, and in particular to the development of sociology, then it becomes a matter of seeing elements of both intellectual fragmentation and synthesis proceeding at the same time. To return to my earlier analogies, we might make a meal of an omelette, chips and peas on the same plate, or whilst our Lego might be an important toy, others are not excluded.

Both processes are essential. The completely integrated person and the completely disintegrated person (if we can imagine such people) are not very attractive propositions - imagine what it would be like to live with either. A fully synthesised sociology would leave no space for development, originality or creativity; in a disintegrated discipline there might be a lot of originality and creativity, but it would have no importance beyond itself. Thus the pull to synthesise is always there, and it should be there.

What does this mean for my criticism of Giddens? I have been highly critical of the synthetic project of structuration theory, arguing that the world is too complex to be grasped by such a project, and I have tried to take it apart. The logic of my argument has taken me further towards the 'disintegrating' position than perhaps I would like, and I suspect this might be necessary when a synthesis such as Giddens's comes to occupy centre stage. At times when fragmentation seems to be dominant, it is perhaps time to emphasise what is common to and what can be connected in alternative positions. Beyond this, however, there is another alternative, the balance which is neither synthesis nor disintegration but which allows the space for both. Giddens placed in this context is entirely a different matter, and it seems to me that he is raising issues, including the possibility of at least a totalising framework, which need to be raised. To take this further, I will return to my discussion of Giddens and modernity.

AGAINST FRAGMENTATION

My criticism of structuration theory was that it was as much a symptom as an understanding or critique of modernity. The dominant trends in modern intellectual life are away from synthesis, towards an acceptance of fragmentation, relativism, over-simplicity, an abandonment of morality. All of these things are apparent in structuration theory even if some of them are denied by the theory. At the same time, it goes against the tendency of modern thought in its attempt to see the whole, in the insistence that we can at least achieve better or less better knowledge of the world and history. It is difficult indeed to see how English-speaking sociology could have maintained any coherence at all without Giddens raising these issues, and I find it difficult to conceive of any social theory that would not find something in his work on which to build. For the time being, at any rate, structuration theory will be the food at the centre of the plate.

Bibliography

This is not an exhaustive bibliography; it contains the works referenced in the text plus a selection of papers by and about Anthony Giddens and aspects of his work that I have found particularly useful.

GIDDENS'S MOST IMPORTANT BOOKS CITED IN THE TEXT

Giddens, A. (1971) *Capitalism and Modern Social Theory*, Cambridge: Cambridge University Press.
—— (1973) *The Class Structure of the Advanced Societies*, London: Hutchinson.
—— (1976) *New Rules of Sociological Method*, London: Hutchinson.
—— (1977) *Studies in Social and Political Theory*, London: Hutchinson.
—— (1979a) *Central Problems in Social Theory*, London: Macmillan.
—— (1981a) *A Contemporary Critique of Historical Materialism: Vol. 1: Power, Property and the State*, London: Macmillan.
—— (1982a) *Profiles and Critiques in Social Theory*, London: Macmillan.
—— (1984) *The Constitution of Society*, Cambridge: Polity Press.
—— (1985a) *A Contemporary Critique of Historical Materialism: Vol. 2: The Nation State and Violence*, Cambridge: Polity Press.
—— (1987a) *Social Theory and Modern Sociology*, Cambridge: Polity Press.
—— (1990) *The Consequences of Modernity*, Cambridge: Polity Press.

OTHER WORKS BY GIDDENS

Giddens, A. (1964) 'Notes on the Concept of Play and Leisure', *Sociological Review* 12: 73–89.
—— (1966) 'A Typology of Suicide', *Archives Europeennes de Sociologie* 7: 276–95.

198 Anthony Giddens

—— (1970a) 'Recent Works on the History of Social Thought', *Archives Europeennes de Sociologie* 11, 130-42.

—— (1970b) 'Recent Works of the Position and Prospects of Contemporary Sociology', *Archives Europeennes de Sociologie* 11: 143-54.

—— (1970c) 'Durkheim as a Review Critic', *Sociological Review* 18: 171-92.

Giddens, A. (ed.) (1971b) *The Sociology of Suicide: A Selection of Readings*, London: Frank Cass & Co. Ltd.

—— (1972a) *Emile Durkheim: Selected Writings*, Cambridge: Cambridge University Press.

Giddens, A. (1972b) *Politics and Sociology in the Thought of Max Weber*, London: Macmillan.

Giddens, A. (ed.) (1974) *Positivism and Sociology*, London: Heinemann.

Giddens, A. (1978) *Durkheim*, London: Fontana.

—— (1979b) 'An Anatomy of the British Ruling Class', *New Society* 50: 8-10.

—— (1981b) 'Agency, Institution and Time-Space Analysis', in K. Knorr-Cetina and A. V. Cicourel (eds): *Advances in Social Theory and Methodology: Towards an Integration of Micro- and Macro-sociologies*, London: Routledge & Kegan Paul.

—— (1981c) 'Modernism and Postmodernism', *New German Critique* 22: 15-18.

—— (1982b) 'A Reply to My Critics', *Theory, Culture and Society* 1 (2): 107-13.

Giddens, A. and Held, D. (eds) (1982c) *Classes, Power and Conflict: Classical and Contemporary Debates*, London: Macmillan.

Giddens, A. (1982d) 'Historical Materialism Today (an interview with Joseph Blucher and Mike Featherstone)', *Theory, Culture and Society* 1 (2): 63-77.

—— (1982e) 'On the Relation of Sociology and Philosophy', in P. Secord (ed) *Explaining Human Behaviour*, London: Sage.

Giddens, A. and MacKenzie, G. (eds) (1982f) *Social Class and the Division of Labour: Essays in Honour of Ilja Neustadt*, Cambridge: Cambridge University Press.

Giddens, A. (1982g) *Sociology: A Brief but Critical Introduction*, London: Macmillan.

—— (1983) 'Comments on the Theory of Structuration', *Journal for the Theory of Social Behaviour* 13: 75-80.

—— (1985b) 'Jurgen Habermas', in Q. Skinner (ed.) *The Return of Grand Theory in the Social Sciences*, Cambridge: Cambridge University Press.

—— (1985c) 'Liberalism and Sociology', *Contemporary Sociology* 14, 320-22.

—— (1985d) 'Marx's Correct Views on Everything (with apologies to L. Kolakowski)', *Theory and Society* 14: 167-73.

—— (1985e) 'Time, Space and Regionalisation', in D. Gregory and J. Urry (eds) *Social Relations and Spatial Structure*, London: Macmillan.

—— (1987b) 'Interview', in B. Mullan *Sociologists on Sociology*, London and Sydney: Croom Helm.

Giddens, A. and Turner, J. (eds) (1987c) *Social Theory Today*, Cambridge: Polity Press.

Giddens, A. (1989a) *Sociology*, Cambridge: Polity Press.

—— (1989b) 'A Reply To My Critics', in D. Held and J. B. Thompson (eds): *Social Theory of Modern Societies: Anthony Giddens and his Critics*, Cambridge: Cambridge University Press.

CRITICISMS AND COMMENTARIES ON GIDDENS'S WORK

Albrow, M. (1990) 'English Channel', *Times Higher Education Supplement* No. 991, 20 April.

Archer, M. (1982) 'Morphogenesis vs. Structuration', *British Journal of Sociology* 33: 455-83.

Ashley, D. (1982) 'Historical Materialism and Social Evolution', *Theory, Culture and Society* 1, (2): 89-91.

Bernstein, R. J. (1989) 'Social Theory as Critique', in D. Held, and J. B. Thompson (eds) *Social Theory of Modern Societies: Anthony Giddens and his Critics*, Cambridge: Cambridge University Press.

Bertilsson, M. (1984) 'The Theory of Structuration: Prospects and Problems', *Acta Sociologica* 27: 339-52.

Betts, K. (1986) 'The Conditions of Action, Power and the Problem of Interests', *Sociological Review* 34, 39-64.

Bhaskar, R. (1983) 'Beef, Structure and Place: notes from a critical naturalist perspective', *Journal of the Theory of Social Behaviour* 13: 81-95.

Boyne, R. (1991) 'Power, Knowledge and Social Theory: The Systematic Misrepresentation of Contemporary French Social Theory in the Work of Anthony Giddens', in C. G. A. Byrant and D. Jary (eds) *Giddens' Theory of Structuration*, London: Routlege.

Bottomore, T. (1990) 'Giddens's View of Historical Materialism', in J. Clark *et al.* (eds) *Anthony Giddens: Consensus and Controversy*, London: The Falmer Press.

Bryant, C. G. A. (1990) 'Sociology without Epistemology? The Case of Giddens' Structuration Theory', unpublished paper presented to XII World Congress of Sociology, Madrid, Sociological Theory Working Group.

Bryant, C. G. A. and Jary, D. (eds) (1991) *Giddens' Theory of Structuration*, London: Routledge.

Callinicos, A. (1985) 'Anthony Giddens: A Contemporary Critique', *Theory and Society* 14: 133-66.

Carlstein, T. (1981) 'The Sociology of Structuration in Time and Space', *Swedish Geographical Yearbook* 57: 41-57.

Clark, J, Modgil, C. and Modgil, F. (eds) (1990) *Anthony Giddens: Consensus and Controversy*, Brighton: Falmer Press.

Cohen, I. J. (1983) 'Breaking New Ground in the Analysis of Capitalism', *Current Sociology* 12: 363-5.

—— (1986) 'The Status of Structuration Theory: A Reply to McLennan', *Theory, Culture and Society* 3 (1), 123-34.

—— (1987) 'Structuration Theory and Social Praxis', in A. Giddens and J. Turner (eds) *Social Theory Today*, Cambridge: Polity Press.

—— (1989) *Structuration Theory: Anthony Giddens and The Constitution of Social Life*, London: Macmillan.

—— (1990) 'Structuration Theory and Social Order: Five Issues in Brief', in J. Clark *et al.* (eds) *Anthony Giddens: Consensus and Controversy*; London: The Falmer Press.

Collins, R. (1983) 'Society As Time Traveller', *Contemporary Sociology* 12: 365-7.

Craib, I. (1986) 'Back to Utopia: Anthony Giddens and Modern Social Theory', *Radical Philosophy* 43: 17-21.

Dallmayr, Fred R. (1982) 'The Theory of Structuration: A Critique in A. Giddens', *Profiles and Critiques in Social Theory*, London: Macmillan.

Gane, M. (1983) 'Anthony Giddens and the Crisis of Social Theory', *Economy and Society* 12: 368-98.

Gregory, D. (1984) 'Space, Time and Politics in Social Theory', *Society and Space* 2: 123-32.

Gregory, D. and Urry, J. (eds) (1985) *Social Relations and Spatial Structures*, London: Macmillan.

Gross, D. (1982) 'Time-Space Relations in Giddens's Social Theory', *Theory, Culture and Society* 1 (2): 83-88.

Hekman, S. (1990) 'Hermeneutics and The Crisis of Social Theory: A Critique of Giddens's Epistemology', in J. Clark *et al.* (eds) *Anthony Giddens: Consensus and Controversy*, London: The Falmer Press.

Held, D. (1982) 'Review of *A Contemporary Critique of Historical Materialism*', *Theory, Culture and Society* 1 (1): 98-102.

Held, D. and Thompson, J. B. (1989) *Social Theory of Modern Societies: Anthony Giddens and His Critics*, Cambridge: Cambridge University Press.

Hirst, P. (1982) 'The Social Theory of Anthony Giddens: A New Syncretism', *Theory, Culture and Society* 2 (2): 78-82.

Jary, D. (1991) 'Society as Time-Traveller: Giddens on Historical Change, Historical Materialism and the Nation-State in World Society', in C. G. A. Bryant and D. Jary (eds) *Giddens' Theory of Structuration*, London: Routledge.

Kilminster, R. (1991) 'Structuration Theory as a World View', in C. G. A. Bryant, and D. Jary, (eds) *Giddens' Theory of Structuration: A Critical Appreciation*; London: Routledge.

Layder, D. (1981) *Structure, Interaction and Social Theory*, London: Routledge and Kegan Paul.

—— (1985) 'Power, Structure and Agency', *Journal for the Theory of Social Behaviour* 15: 131-49.

Livesay, J. (1985) 'Normative Grounding and Praxis', *Sociological Theory* 3: 66-76.

McLennan, G. (1984) 'Critical or Positive Theory: A Comment on The

Status of Anthony Giddens's Social Theory', *Theory, Culture and Society* 2 (2): 123-30.

—— (1990) 'The Temporal and the Temporising in Structuration Theory', in J. Clark *et al.* (eds) *Anthony Giddens: Consensus and Controversy*, London: The Falmer Press.

Mouzelis, N. (1989) 'Restructuring Structuration Theory', *Sociological Review* 37, 613-35.

Outhwaite, W. (1990) 'Agency and Structure', in I. Clark *et al.* (eds) *Anthony Giddens: Consensus and Controversy*, London: The Falmer Press.

Saunders, P. (1989) 'Space, Urbanism and the Created Environment', in D. Held and J. B. Thompson (eds): *Social Theory of Modern Societies: Anthony Giddens and his Critics*, Cambridge: Cambridge University Press.

Sayer, D. (1990) 'Reinventing the Wheel: Anthony Giddens, Karl Marx and Social Change', in J. Clark *et al.* (eds) *Anthony Giddens: Consensus and Controversy*, London: The Falmer Press.

Sica, A. (1986) 'Locating the 17th Book of Giddens', *Contemporary Sociology* 15: 344-46.

Smith, C. W. (1983) 'A Case-study of Structuration: The Pure-bred Beef Business', *Journal for the Theory of Social Behaviour* 13: 3-18.

Smith, D. (1982) 'Put Not Your Trust in Princes', *Theory, Culture and Society* 1 (2): 93-9.

Smith, J. W. and Turner, B. S. (1986) 'Constructing Social Theory and Constituting Society', *Theory, Culture and Society* 3 (2): 125-33.

Stinchcombe, A. (1990) 'Milieu and Structure Updated: A Critique of the Theory of Structuration', in J. Clark *et al.* (eds) *Anthony Giddens: Consensus and Controversy*, London: The Falmer Press.

Stones, R. (1991) 'Strategic Context Analysis: A New Research Strategy for Structuration Theory', *Sociology* 25 (3).

Thompson, J. B. (1984) 'Rethinking History: For and Against Marx', *Philosophy of the Social Sciences* 14: 543-51.

—— (1989) 'The Theory of Structuration', in D. Held and J. B. Thompson (eds) *Social Theory of Modern Societies: Anthony Giddens and his Critics*, Cambridge: Cambridge University Press.

Thrift, N. (1983) 'On the Determination of Action in Space and Time', *Society and Space* 1: 23-57.

—— (1985) 'Bear and Mouse or Bear and Tree? Anthony Giddens's Reconstitution of Social Theory', *Sociology* 19: 609-23.

Turner, J. H. (1986) 'The Theory of Structuration', *American Journal of Sociology* 91: 969-77.

—— (1990) 'Giddens's Analysis of Functionalism: A Critique', in J. Clark *et al.* (eds) *Anthony Giddens: Consensus and Controversy*, London: The Falmer Press.

Urry, J. (1977) 'Review of *New Rules of Sociological Method*', *Sociological Review* 25: 911-15.

—— (1982) 'Duality of Structure: Some Critical Issues', *Theory, Culture and Society* 1 (2): 100-6.

—— (1991) 'Time and Space in Giddens' Social Theory', in C. G. A.

Bryant, and D. Jary (eds) *Giddens' Theory of Structuration: A Critical Appreciation*; London: Routledge.

Willmott, H. C. (1986) 'Unconscious Sources in the Theory of the Subject: An Exploration and Critique of Giddens's Dualistic Models of Action and Personality', *Journal for the Theory of Social Behaviour* 16: 105-21.

Wright, E. O. (1989) 'Models of Historical Trajectory: an assessment of Giddens's Critique of Marxism', in D. Held and J. B. Thompson (eds) *Social Theory of Modern Societies: Anthony Giddens and his Critics*, Cambridge: Cambridge University Press.

OTHER REFERENCES AND BACKGROUND READING

Alexander, J. (ed.) (1985) *Neofunctionalism*, London: Sage.

Althusser, L. (1989) *For Marx*, London: Allen Lane: The Penguin Press.

Anderson, P. (1968) 'Components of the National Culture', *New Left Review* 50: 3-57.

—— (1974a) *Passages From Antiquity to Feudalism*, London: New Left Books.

—— (1974b) *Lineages of the Absolutist State*, London: New Left Books.

—— (1990) 'A Culture in Counterflow - 1', *New Left Review* 180: 41-78.

Becker, E. (1975) *The Denial of Death*, New York: The Free Press.

Bhaskar, R. (1979) *The Possibility of Naturalism*, Brighton: Harvester.

Bion, W. R. (1959) 'Attacks on Linking', *International Journal of Psychoanalysis* 40: 308-15.

Blumer, H. (1969) *Symbolic Interactionism: Perspective and Method*, Englewood Cliffs, N.J.: Prentice Hall.

Buckley, W. (1967) *Sociology and Modern Systems Theory*, Englewood Cliffs, N.J.: Prentice-Hall.

Buckley, W. (ed.) (1968) *Modern Systems Research for the Behavioural Scientist*, Chicago: Aldine.

Cohen, G. A. (1978) *Karl Marx's Theory of History: A Defence*, Oxford: Clarendon Press.

—— (1982) 'Functional Explanation, Consequence Explanation and Marxism', *Inquiry* 25: 27-56.

Craib, I. (1987) 'The Psychodynamics of Theory', *Free Associations* 10: 32-58.

—— (1990) *Psychoanalysis and Social Theory: The Limits of Sociology*, Amherst, Ma.: University of Massachusetts Press.

Eisenstadt, S. N. (1963) *The Political Systems of Empires*, Glencoe: The Free Press.

Elster, J. (1979) *Ulysses and the Sirens*, Cambridge: Cambridge University Press.

Erikson, E. (1977) *Childhood and Society*, London: Triad/Paladin.

Feyerabend, P. (1975) *Against Method*, London: New Left Books.

Foucault, M. (1979) *Discipline and Punish*, Harmondsworth: Penguin.

Frosh, S. (1989a) 'Melting into Air: Psychoanalysis and Social Experience', *Free Associations* 16: 7-30.

—— (1989b) 'On Narcissism', *Free Associations* 18: 22-48.

Garfinkel, H. (1967) *Studies in Ethnomethodology*, Englewood Cliffs, N.J.: Prentice Hall.

Gerth, H. and Mills, C. Wright (1953) *Character and Social Structure*, New York: Harcourt Brace.

Goffman, E. (1974) *Frame Analysis*, New York: Harper Row.

Gouldner, A. W. (1970) *The Coming Crisis of Western Sociology*, New York: Basic Books.

Hagerstrand, T. (1975) 'Space, Time and Human Conditions', in A. Karquist (ed.) *Dynamic Allocation of Urban Space*, Farnborough: Saxon House.

—— (1976) *Innovation as a Spatial Process*, Chicago: University of Chicago Press.

Hesse, M. (1974) *The Structure of Scientific Inference*, London.

Inglis, F. (1982) *Radical Earnestness: English Social Theory 1880–1980*, Oxford: Martin Robertson.

Klein, M. (1986) 'Notes on Some Schizoid Mechanisms', in J. Mitchell (ed.) *The Selected Melanie Klein*, Harmondsworth: Penguin.

Kuhn, T. (1962) *The Structure of Scientific Revolutions*, Chicago: University of Chicago Press.

Knorr-Cetina, K. and Cicourel, A. V. (1981) *Advances in Social Theory and Methodology: Towards an Integration of Micro- and Macro-sociologies*, London: Routledge & Kegan Paul.

Laing, R. D. (1960) *The Divided Self*, Harmondsworth: Penguin.

Lasch, C. (1977) *Haven in a Heartless World*, New York: Basic Books.

—— (1980) *The Culture of Narcissism: American Life in an Age of Diminishing Expectations*, London: Sphere Books.

—— (1984) *The Minimal Self: Psychic Survival in Troubled Times*, London: Picador.

Luhmann, N. (1984) *Soziale Systeme*, Frankfurt: Suhrkamp.

Mann, M. (1986) *The Sources of Social Power Vol. 1: A History of Power from the Beginning to A.D. 1760*, Cambridge: Cambridge University Press.

Maruyama, M. (1963) 'The Second Cybernetics: Deviation Amplifying Mutual Causal Processes', *American Scientist* 51: 164–79.

Marx, K. (1973) *Grundrisse*, Harmondsworth: Penguin Books.

Merton, R. K. (1968) *Social Theory and Social Structure*, Glencoe, Illinois: Free Pass.

Mills, C. Wright (1959) *The Sociological Imagination*, New York: Oxford University Press.

Mullan, B. (1987) *Sociologists on Sociology*, London: Croom Helm.

Pred, A. (ed.) (1981) *Space and Time in Geography: Essays Dedicated to Torsten Hagerstrand*, Lund Studies in Geography Series B: Human Geography, Lund: CWK Gleerup.

Rex, J. (1983) 'British Sociology 1960–80: An Essay', *Social Forces* 61: 999–1009.

Runciman, W. G. (1983) *A Treatise on Social Theory Vol. I: The Methodology of Social Theory*, Cambridge: Cambridge University Press.

—— (1989) *A Treatise on Social Theory Vol II: Substantive Social Theory*, Cambridge: Cambridge University Press.

Sartre, J-P. (1976) *The Critique of Dialectical Reason*, London: New Left Books.

Saussure, F. De (1966) *Course in General Linguistics*, New York: McGraw-Hill.

Scheff, T. (1966) *Being Mentally Ill: A Sociological Theory*, New York: Aldine 1966.

Winch, P. (1958) *The Idea of a Social Science*, London: Routledge & Kegan Paul.

Winnicott, D. W. (1964) *The Child, the Family and the Outside World*, Harmondsworth: Penguin.

Index